Conquer Grammar

Table of Contents

Introduction

This book is designed to help students have a better understanding of grammar, the fundamental organizing principle of language. The standards for most states as well as the Common Core State Standards require that students "Demonstrate command of the conventions of standard English grammar usage when writing and speaking." Students who understand how to use proper grammar are better able to say what they mean when writing and speaking.

Each of the 84 worksheets in this book reinforces a grade-appropriate grammar topic. The book is organized by parts of speech and other key topics. The goal is to equip students with an understanding of grammar so they can communicate more effectively.

How to Use This Book

Here are just a few of the many ways you can use this resource.

Grammar Mini-Lessons: The most basic way to use this book is as a source of grammar mini-lessons. Write the grammar rule on the board. You can copy this straight from the gray box found on each worksheet. Introduce the rule, explain it, and then give examples. See if students can come up with their own examples. Then have students complete the worksheet. You can ask students to complete the worksheets individually or with partners, depending on ability levels. Check for understanding.

Grammar Reinforcement: After you have taught students a particular grammar rule, you can use these pages to give students the practice they need to reinforce their knowledge of the skill.

Grammar Assessment: The worksheets can serve as a formative assessment tool to show you where students might need additional teaching. Worksheets can also serve as a final assessment to confirm that students have mastered a particular rule.

Beyond the Book

There are a myriad of ways in which you can extend the lessons in this book. The goal is to keep the learning fun and interactive. Here are several ideas to get you started.

- Find examples of grammar rules you are studying in books you are reading in class. Point out these examples to students. Then send students on a scavenger hunt to find examples themselves. You can expand the search area to books students read at home and in magazines, newspapers, notices around school, advertisements, and anywhere there is a written word. The more places students see the rule being used, the better.

- Ask students to practice using specific grammar rules in their own writing. For example, if you are studying a particular type of punctuation, have students use that punctuation in their writing. They can even go back and revise old work using knowledge gained from new grammar rules.

- Build a grammar "Wall of Shame" where you post examples of writing—usually from advertisements—where grammar rules were ignored, often to humorous effect. Encourage students to look for examples to add to the Wall of Shame. You might want to post an example you can easily find on the Internet, "Let's eat Grandpa" versus "Let's eat, Grandpa," and point out that grammar can save lives.

- Create a short daily exercise in which students are asked to use a recently learned grammar rule to correct a sentence that is written on the board. Students love correcting others' mistakes!

- Set up grammar stations with worksheets that cover a different rule at each station. Have students work in small groups to add one or two new questions to the worksheet at each station. Make a quiz out of the student-written questions.

Key Tips for Teaching English Learners

The rules of grammar vary between different languages. This can make learning English grammar particularly difficult for English Learners. It is helpful to know where the grammar rules between languages differ so much as to cause a fair amount of confusion. Here are some of those areas.

Word Order	In languages such as Spanish, Farsi, Arabic, and Korean, word order in sentences may vary from that of English.
Verbs	In English, verbs are inflected for person and number. (*Everyone cooks food. She has a large cat.*) Verbs are not inflected for person and number in Vietnamese, Hmong, Korean, Cantonese, and Mandarin. (*Everyone cook food. She have large cat.*)
Nouns	Nouns and adjectives use different forms in English. (*They felt safe in their home. They were concerned about safety.*) In Spanish, Hmong, Cantonese, and Mandarin, speakers use the same form for nouns and adjectives. (*They felt safety in their home.*)
Possessive Nouns	In English, we add an apostrophe and *s* to most singular nouns, or an apostrophe only to proper, plural names that end in *s*, to show possession. In Spanish, Vietnamese, Hmong, and Tagalog, possession is shown using *of*. It is always *of Holly*, not *Holly's*.
Plural Nouns	Nouns become plural after a number greater than one in English. (*We go home in two weeks. They are bringing five shirts.*) In Vietnamese, Hmong, Tagalog, Korean, Cantonese, Mandarin, and Farsi, there is no change in the noun following a number. (*We go home in two week. They are bringing five shirt.*)
Adjectives	Adjectives precede the nouns they modify in English (*the blue flower*). In Spanish, Vietnamese, Hmong, Farsi, and Arabic, adjectives follow the nouns they modify (*the flower blue*).
Pronouns	In English, there is a distinction between subject and object pronouns. (*He gave it to me. We spent time with her.*) In Spanish, Vietnamese, Hmong, Cantonese, Mandarin, and Farsi, there is no distinction. (*He gave it to I. We spent time with she.*)
Prepositions	The use of prepositions in other languages differs from those used in English. (English: *The movie is on the DVD.* Spanish: *The movie is in the DVD.*)
Articles	Indefinite articles are used consistently in English. (*She is a brilliant scientist. He is an electrician.*) In Spanish, Hmong, Tagalog, Cantonese, and Mandarin, indefinite articles can be omitted. (*She is brilliant scientist. He is electrician.*)

Proper Nouns

Common nouns name general people, places, or things. Proper nouns name specific people, places, or things. Each main word of a proper noun should begin with a capital letter.

Common Noun	Proper Noun
boy	Patrick Brown
city	Salt Lake City
museum	Baseball Hall of Fame

Complete the chart by writing a proper noun for each common noun. Use correct capitalization.

Common Nouns	Proper Nouns
country	
mountain	
author	
state	
holiday	
ocean	
national park	
continent	
president	
city	

Conquer Grammar • Grade 6 • © Newmark Learning, LLC

Plural Nouns

A plural noun names more than one person, place, or thing. Add **s** to the end of most nouns to make them plural. For nouns ending in **x, z, s, sh,** or **ch,** add **-es**. For nouns ending in a consonant and **y**, change the **y** to **i** and add **-es**. For nouns ending in **f** or **fe**, change the last letter to **v** and then add **-es**.

Singular Noun	Plural Noun
cat	cats
lady	ladies
fly	flies
loaf	loaves
life	lives

**Write the plural form of the noun in the parentheses ( )
to complete each sentence.**

1. Don't you agree that Aunt Gloria throws the best _____? (party)

2. My little brothers jumped into the piles of _____ in the yard. (leaf)

3. Grandmother polished her antique silver spoons, forks, and _____. (knife)

4. We saw the newest _____ in the pasture. (calf)

5. Benjamin showed me his huge collection of _____. (penny)

6. The wild horses' _____ made a thundering noise as the herd ran by. (hoof)

7. The _____ were packed with books. (shelf)

8. The _____ jumped onto the chair. (puppy)

Irregular Plural Nouns

The plural form of some nouns is irregular because there are no clear spelling rules to follow when forming the plural. Sometimes a noun's spelling doesn't change at all.

Singular Noun	Plural Noun
man	men
foot	feet
offspring	offspring
salmon	salmon
louse	lice

Circle the plural noun in the parentheses ( ) that correctly completes each sentence. If necessary, use a dictionary for help.

1. We caught many (trout, trouts) on our last fishing trip.

2. My friend in Canada often sees a flock of (goose, geese) in her yard.

3. Once in awhile, she may see several (moose, meese) from her window.

4. The Saturday matinee was filled with hundreds of (children, childs).

5. Do you think we will see some (deer, deers) grazing in the meadow?

6. The (workmans, workmen) helped build the tallest building in town.

7. Despite being very excited, the (people, persons) in the crowd didn't make much noise.

8. The (woman, women) worked together to repair the broken fence.

Possessive Nouns

A possessive noun tells who or what owns something.
Use **'s** to show possession for one person, place, or thing.
   The toy belongs to the cat. It is the **cat's** toy.

Use **s'** to show possession for more than one person, place, or thing.
   The cat belongs to my two sisters. It is my **sisters'** cat.

Use **'s** to show possession for a noun with an irregular plural form.
   The **schoolchildren's** teacher was absent today.

Circle the possessive noun in each sentence. Then write whether it is singular or plural.

1. My grandfather's truck was filled with camping supplies. _____

2. The geese's honking could be heard from a mile away. _____

3. All of the tourists' photos were of the same landmark. _____

4. Unfortunately, the women's team practice was canceled today. _____

5. I couldn't believe how long that giraffe's neck really was! _____

6. The trees' fruit was ready to be harvested. _____

Name _____ Date _____

Present Perfect Tense

The present perfect tense tells about an action that starts in the past and continues into the present. It can also tell about changes or experiences that happen over a period of time. The present perfect tense uses the helping verbs **has** or **have** with the past tense of a main verb.

Lindsay **has loved** to sing as long as we all can remember.

Winston and Walter **have played** on the soccer team since last year.

Rewrite each sentence with the present perfect tense of the verb in the parentheses ( ).

1. I (wash) my own laundry since I was nine years old.

_____

2. Mom thinks you (outgrow) your bicycle, and she said I can have it.

_____

3. Richard (complete) his hike along the Appalachian Trail.

_____

4. Daryll and Diana (learn) to snowboard in time for their vacation.

_____

5. With this trip, Jason's dad (visit) every national park in California.

_____

6. Because she will visit France, Rory (decide) to learn French.

_____

7. The construction team (work) hard to complete the bridge within budget.

_____

8. The twins (open) all of their presents and now we will eat cake and ice cream.

_____

Conquer Grammar • Grade 6 • © Newmark Learning, LLC

Perfect Tenses

The present perfect tense tells about an action that starts in the past and continues into the present. It can also tell about changes or experiences that happen over a period of time. The present perfect tense uses the helping verbs **has** or **have** with the past tense of a main verb.
  Present perfect: William **has played** the drums and clarinet since September.

The past perfect tense tells about an action that starts and ends in the past. The past perfect tense uses the helping verb **had** with the past tense of a main verb.
  Past perfect: By the end of summer, he **had learned** to play the violin.

The future perfect tense tells about an action that starts in the past and continues into the future. The future perfect tense uses the helping verb **will have** with the past tense of a main verb.
  Future perfect: By next year, he **will have mastered** three instruments.

Rewrite each sentence with the indicated tense of the underlined verb.

1. My mom <u>serve</u> perfect meatballs since I can remember. (present perfect)

_____

2. Nana <u>teach</u> her to make them by the time Mom was my age. (past perfect)

_____

3. My grandmother <u>live</u> with us for the past three months. (present perfect)

_____

4. After next week, Mom and Dad <u>renew</u> their wedding vows. (future perfect)

_____

5. I hope in twenty years, I <u>find</u> a true love like theirs. (future perfect)

_____

6. Nana <u>discover</u> the recipe written on her mother's tattered index card. (past perfect)

_____

Literary Present Tense

When describing the events that occur in a story or a play, use the present tense or the literary present.

In *Annie,* the main character **is** a young girl who **lives** in an orphanage.

For each passage, underline the form of the verb in the parentheses ( ) that is in the literary present.

1. In *Romeo and Juliet*, one of Shakespeare's most famous plays, the two main characters meet at a party and (fell, fall) in love. The problem is that their families (hate, hated) each other. Romeo and Juliet (know, knew) they will not be allowed to marry. However, Friar Laurence kindly (helped, helps) them marry in secret.
Then something terrible (happened, happens). The day after the wedding, Romeo (kills, killed) Juliet's cousin in a duel. In the morning he (is, was) forced to leave Juliet. Romeo (cannot, could not) return to the city, or else he will be put to death.

2. In *Because of Winn-Dixie* by Kate DiCamillo, ten-year-old Opal Buloni (has, had) just moved to a new town in Florida. She (was, is) lonely and missing her mother who left when Opal was only three years old. Opal (is wondering, was wondering) how she is going to make it through the long, hot summer when she (finds, found) a big dog in a Winn-Dixie grocery store. She (named, names) the dog Winn-Dixie and (takes, took) him home to meet her father.

Name _____ Date _____

Literary Present Tense

When describing the events that occur in a story or a play, use the present tense or the literary present.

In *The Giver*, Jonas **is** a boy who **stores** his community's memories.

Complete the essay. Write the literary present tense form of the verb in the parentheses ( ).

In the novel *Tuck Everlasting,* by Natalie Babbitt, the members of

the Tuck family have eternal life because they _____ water from a
                                                    (to drink)

magic spring. The family _____ from place to place. They _____
                          (to move)   (lived)

so quietly that their neighbors don't realize that there is something odd

about the family.

Then ten-year-old Winnie Foster accidentally _____ the Tucks'
                                              (to discover)

secret. The Tucks _____ to explain why remaining the same age
                    (to try)

forever isn't as wonderful as it _____. The plot thickens when a
                                  (to seem)

stranger _____. He has a plan. He _____ to market the spring
          (to arrive)   (wanted)
water.

Verb Tenses

Present tense verbs tell about something that is happening right now. Past tense verbs tell about something that has already happened. Future tense verbs tell about something that will happen at a later time.

Present: I **exercise** after school.
Past: Yesterday, I **exercised** with my friend.
Future: I **will exercise** every day next week.

For each sentence, determine when the action is happening. Choose the verb in parentheses ( ) that correctly completes the sentence and write it on the line.

1. I am going to the community center, and I _____ with my friends.

    (will study, studied)

2. Tomorrow, we _____ out for dinner, and then we will visit Mara.

    (will go, went)

3. I _____ a sandwich even though I had already eaten lunch.

    (eat, ate)

4. When Mr. Sansone arrives, he _____ out the awards.

    (will give, gives)

5. The Nile River, which is in Africa, _____ south of the Equator and flows north.   (rises, rose)

6. The two rivals _____ to resolve their differences.

    (are meeting, met)

7. In the novel, the main character is stunned when she first _____ her long-lost friend.   (sees, saw)

Shifts in Verb Tense

Present tense verbs tell about something that is happening right now. Past tense verbs tell about something that has already happened. Future tense verbs tell about something that will happen at a later time. Change tenses to describe actions that happen at different times.

The children **hiked** all day and **are** now resting by the campfire.

Underline the verbs that shift tenses in each sentence.

1. The sun rose early, but the air is still cool.

2. I will stay in my sleeping bag until I hear the other campers talking.

3. We heard strange sounds last night and now everyone thinks there are bears around.

4. I slept well last night, however, I will sleep poorly tonight!

5. Mila ran a race, and now she is resting.

Write the correct form of the verb in the parentheses ( )
to complete each sentence.

6. Today was rainy, but we hope tomorrow _____ sunny.
(to be)

7. We started the campfire in the morning and it still _____ brightly.
(burn)

8. I brought my dog, Rex, on the trip because my friends _____ him a lot.
(like)

9. We love being in the wilderness, but we _____ home later today.
(return)

Shifts in Verb Tense

Present tense verbs tell about something that is happening right now. Past tense verbs tell about something that has already happened. Future tense verbs tell about something that will happen at a later time. Change tenses to describe actions that happen at different times.

We **are** surprised that the movie **had** a happy ending.
The staff **will pop** more popcorn because they just **sold** the last bag.

Circle the correct verb to complete each sentence.

1. I called my friend to ask if she (went, will go) with me to see the movie.

2. I will want company if the movie (was, is) scary!

3. We arrived late, but the trailers (are, will be) still running.

4. I usually walk to school, but yesterday I (ride, rode) my bike.

5. After I eat dinner, I (will play, played) the piano.

6. We played basketball this morning, but now we (are, were) resting.

7. I already ate my lunch, so I (buy, will buy) a snack.

8. As soon as I get to the beach, I (will jump, jump) in the ocean.

9. We will play checkers while we (wait, will wait) for the storm to pass.

Shifts in Verb Tense

Present tense verbs tell about something that is happening right now. Past tense verbs tell about something that has already happened. Future tense verbs tell about something that will happen at a later time. Change tenses to describe actions that happen at different times.

The sky **is** clear now, but maybe it **will rain** later.

Choose the correct verb in the parentheses ( ). Write it on the line.

1. After we eat lunch, we (walked, will walk) the dogs. _____

2. The dogs played, and now they (are, were) snoozing. _____

3. I finished my book report, and now I (played, play) my guitar. _____

4. We planted bulbs that (bloomed, will bloom) in March. _____

Rewrite the passage. Use the literary present tense of the verbs in the parentheses ( ).

Encyclopedia Brown books (to feature) a boy detective, Leroy Brown. His nickname is "Encyclopedia," because he (to be) very intelligent and well-read. Most of the books in the series (to begin) with Leroy having dinner with his father, the police chief of a small town. The chief (to describe) his current case to his son. Leroy (to ask) a question or two. Then he (to solve) the mystery right at the dinner table.

_____

_____

_____

_____

_____

Subject-Verb Agreement

The subject of a sentence is a noun that tells who or what the sentence is about. The verb tells what the subject does. The subject and the verb of a sentence must agree. A singular subject takes a singular verb. A plural subject, including a compound subject, takes a plural verb.

Singular Subject: A <u>student</u> from our class **is** in the talent show.
Plural Subject: <u>Ms. Jeffries and Mr. Thomas</u> often **attend** the meetings.
Compound Subject: The <u>committee members</u> **hope** lots of students will participate.

Underline the subject of each sentence. Then choose the verb in the parentheses ( ) that agrees with the subject and write it on the line.

1. The list of story-starters _____ on the board.

(is, are)

2. Dean and Maisha _____ co-chairs of the advisory board.

(is, are)

3. The members of the board _____ to meet again next week.

(has agreed, have agreed)

4. Mark and I _____ excited to meet our favorite ice hockey player.

(was, were)

5. One of the shirts _____ a large, and two are mediums.

(is, are)

6. I _____ to the observatory tomorrow night.

(am going, is going)

7. We _____ why you are frustrated about the results.

(understands, understand)

8. Rita and Drew _____ to write a letter to the editor about the issue.

(intends, intend)

Name _____ Date _____

Subject-Verb Agreement

The subject of a sentence is a noun that tells who or what the sentence is about. The verb tells what the subject does. The subject and the verb of a sentence must agree. A singular subject takes a singular verb. A plural subject, including a compound subject, takes a plural verb.

Singular Subject: The list of suggested books **is** online.
Plural Subject: Hardbacks and paperbacks of all genres **are** available in our library.
Compound Subject: Louise and May **take** out books often.

Underline the subject of each sentence. Then choose the verb in the parentheses ( ) that agrees with the subject and write it on the line.

1. Mary and Celine _____ the strongest players on our team.
(is, are)

2. The teammates _____ in favor of Saturday practice.
(has voted, have voted)

3. The schedule of after-school clubs _____ yesterday.
(was announced, were announced)

4. Before a Spanish test, Melissa and I usually _____ each other on vocabulary. (quizzes, quiz)

5. Two of the students _____ to sing a solo.
(is going, are going)

6. The administrators _____ every Thursday afternoon.
(meets, meet)

7. The lesson topics for the next two weeks _____ online.
(has been posted, have been posted)

Name _____ Date _____

Subject-Verb Agreement

The subject of a sentence is a noun that tells who or what the sentence is about. The verb tells what the subject does. The subject and the verb of a sentence must agree. A singular subject takes a singular verb. A plural subject, including a compound subject, takes a plural verb.

Singular Subject: <u>Marty</u> **goes** to the store.

Plural Subject: <u>We</u> **are** thrilled to be invited to the championship game.

Compound Subject: <u>You and I</u> **have** lunch at noon.

Complete each sentence. Circle the verb in the parentheses ( ) that agrees with the subject of the sentence and write it on the line.

1. All players _____ to be on the field at 11 a.m. (is, are)

2. Nyla, who is my neighbor, and I _____ known each other since we were in the first grade. (has, have)

3. An elephant _____ a very intelligent animal. (is, are)

4. Mabel, who's on the school paper, and I _____ interviewed the custodian. (has, have)

5. I _____ to visit my grandfather on Tuesday. (want, wants)

6. Maura, Kelly, and Rahim _____ running for class president. (is, are)

7. We _____ understand your perspective, but we disagree. (does, do)

8. Shayla and I _____ excited to meet our favorite author. (was, were)

Subject-Verb Agreement

The subject of a sentence is a noun that tells who or what the sentence is about. The verb tells what the subject does. The subject and the verb of a sentence must agree. A singular subject takes a singular verb. A plural subject, including a compound subject, takes a plural verb.

Singular Subject: <u>Molly</u> **takes** the city bus home.
Plural Subject: <u>Edgar and Bob</u> **take** it, too.
Compound Subject: <u>They</u> **will walk** next week.

Circle the verb in the parentheses ( ) that agrees with the subject of the sentence. Then write it on the line.

1. They _____ ready when you are. (is, are)

2. You _____ the stopwatch. (has, have)

3. Lisette and I _____ volunteering at the animal shelter. (am, are)

4. A puppy rarely _____ still for more than five minutes. (sit, sits)

5. You still _____ not realize the depth of the problem. (does, do)

6. Alia _____ bringing beverages to the picnic. (am, is)

7. Rocco and Mia _____ almost home when it began to rain. (was, were)

8. It _____ time to write a clever story. (take, takes)

9. A tutor _____ a student with homework. (help, helps)

10. I like to _____ out for lunch. (go, goes)

Subject-Verb Agreement

The subject of a sentence is a noun that tells who or what the sentence is about. The verb tells what the subject does. The subject and the verb of a sentence must agree. A singular subject takes a singular verb. A plural subject, including a compound subject, takes a plural verb.

Singular Subject: <u>Alejandro</u> **rehearses** for the play every Monday and Thursday.
Plural Subject: <u>Kyle and Misha</u> **are** in charge of costumes.
Compound Subject: <u>Nicky</u>, who is my best friend, <u>and I</u> **are** in the band.

Complete each sentence. Choose the verb in the parentheses ( ) that agrees with the subject of the sentence and write it on the line.

1. The clarinet players in the band _____ together on Saturday.

(practices, practice)

2. The president _____ that he will address the nation.

(says, say)

3. The director of the event _____ a round of applause.

(deserves, deserve)

4. Three of the fish _____ striped and one is solid orange.

(is, are)

5. The fans who watched the game _____ that it was very disappointing.

(agrees, agree)

6. All the neighbors who donated _____ warm clothing.

(has brought, have brought)

7. Everybody _____ in a different way.

(contribute, contributes)

Subject-Verb Agreement

The subject of a sentence is a noun that tells who or what the sentence is about. The verb tells what the subject does. The subject and the verb of a sentence must agree. A singular subject takes a singular verb. A plural subject, including a compound subject, takes a plural verb.

Singular Subject: The list of reference books **is** in your folder.
Plural Subject: Victor and Luis **want** to go to the playoff game.
Compound Subject: Physicians **agree** that learning new things is good for your brain.

Rewrite each sentence with correct subject-verb agreement.

1. The historians speaks at the museum today.

_____

2. The field hockey players practices in the upper field.

_____

3. The citizens of Springfield has a new mayor.

_____

4. Margie and Kevin is at the train station.

_____

5. The best bands in the city marches in the parade.

_____

6. The chickens was running through the yard.

_____

7. My sister decide what to watch.

_____

Subject Pronouns

A pronoun is a word that takes the place of a noun. **I**, **you**, **she**, **he**, **it**, **we**, and **they** are subject pronouns. Use a subject pronoun when a pronoun is the subject of a sentence.

Incorrect: Her is my friend.
Correct: She is my friend.

Incorrect: My brother and **me** walk the dog twice a day.
Correct: My brother and **I** walk the dog twice a day.

Circle the correct subject pronoun in the parentheses ( ) to complete each sentence.

1. (Her, She) and Isabella are out riding skateboards.

2. Klaus and (I, me) will go to the library with you on Thursday.

3. (Him, He) and (me, I) are building a doghouse.

4. (They, Them) and the other tourists boarded the bus at dawn.

Circle the incorrect pronoun in each sentence.
Then rewrite the sentence with the correct subject pronoun.

5. Us and the mayor attended the grand opening.

_____

6. Gil and me decided to work on the puzzle together.

_____

7. Suki and her made a cake.

_____

8. My sister and me play board games.

_____

Name _____ Date _____

Object Pronouns

A pronoun is a word that takes the place of a noun. **Me**, **you**, **him**, **her**, **it**, **us**, and **them** are object pronouns. Use an object pronoun when a pronoun is the object of a verb or a preposition.

Incorrect: The art teacher encouraged Samantha and **I**.
Correct: The art teacher encouraged Samantha and **me**.

Incorrect: This is an important moment for us and **they**.
Correct: This is an important moment for us and **them**.

Circle the correct object pronoun in the parentheses ( ) to complete each sentence.

1. Marina is writing a story about (he, him) and his brother.

2. Jamie rides the subway with my friend and (I, me).

3. Finn sent letters to you and (we, us).

4. That shouldn't be a matter of (we, us) against (them, they).

Circle the incorrect pronoun or pronouns in each sentence. Then rewrite the sentence with the correct object pronoun.

5. Angel went to the play with Cory and I.

_____

6. Mr. Lu coached he and her.

_____

7. Ava gave Nora and I some fruit.

_____

8. Remember to text she and I.

_____

Possessive Pronouns

Pronouns take the place of nouns. A possessive pronoun shows who or what owns something. **My**, **mine**, **your**, **yours**, **her**, **hers**, **his**, **its**, **our**, **ours**, **their**, and **theirs** are possessive pronouns. A possessive pronoun should never have an apostrophe.

This is not **my** backpack. That red one is **mine**.
This dog is **theirs**. I'm taking it back to **their** house.

Circle the possessive pronoun or pronouns in the parentheses ( ) that correctly complete each sentence.

1. The dog chased (its, their) toy.

2. Andy unlocked the door of (his, hers) house.

3. Craig, is this binder (yours, your)?

4. I would like (my, mine) notes back in an hour, please.

5. The two friends decided to eat (their, theirs) lunches together.

6. I finished (mine, my) ice cream. Are you done with (your, yours)?

7. We can have the reunion at (your, yours) house or (our, ours).

8. That dark green backpack is (my, mine), but the green one is (her, hers).

9. The students claimed the library study room as (theirs, their) from
   1 p.m. to 3 p.m.

10. I see that (my, mine) plant needs more water, for (its, their) leaves are
    turning brown.

Name _____ Date _____

Possessive Pronouns

Pronouns take the place of nouns. A possessive pronoun shows who or what owns something. **My**, **mine**, **your**, **yours**, **her**, **hers**, **his**, **its**, **our**, **ours**, **their**, and **theirs** are possessive pronouns. A possessive pronoun should never have an apostrophe.

We have **our** tickets. These three are **ours**.
Her seat is in row B. The seat on the aisle is **hers**.

Circle the correct possessive pronoun. Then write it on the line.

1. Luisa spoke of _____ adventures in the Arctic. (her, hers)

2. Mrs. O'Malley said I could have an extra day to write _____ paper. (my, mine)

3. Jamal turned to me and asked, "Is this notebook mine or _____?" (your, yours)

4. My family moved into _____ new house last month. (our, ours)

5. The cats treated the orphaned kitten as if it were _____. (their, theirs)

For each pair of sentences, circle the possessive pronoun in the first sentence and complete the second sentence with the correct form of the same pronoun.

6. These are our ideas. These ideas are _____.

7. Is this apple yours? Is this _____ apple?

8. That scarf looks just like my scarf. That scarf looks just like _____.

Possessive Pronouns

Pronouns take the place of nouns. A possessive pronoun shows who or what owns something. **My**, **mine**, **your**, **yours**, **her**, **hers**, **his**, **its**, **our**, **ours**, **their**, and **theirs** are possessive pronouns. A possessive pronoun should never have an apostrophe. A contraction always has an apostrophe. Possessive pronouns and contractions are frequently confused.

Possessive Pronoun	**Contraction**
its	it's (it is)
your	you're (you are)
their	they're (they are)
whose	who's (who is)

Complete each sentence. Write the contraction and the possessive pronoun in the parentheses ( ) on the correct line.

1. If you miss _____ connection, _____ going to be late.

(you're, your)

2. Did you say _____ riding _____ surfboards in a competition?

(they're, their)

3. _____ e-mail asked, "_____ your favorite actor?"

(Who's, Whose)

4. Stephen and Darin said _____ calling _____ dad to

come pick them up.   (their, they're)

5. _____ suitcase is this? _____ going to use the treadmill?

(Who's, Whose)

6. Ms. Chen said that _____ going to lend her _____ book.

(you're, your)

7. I think _____ unlucky that I dropped the phone and broke

_____ screen.   (its, it's)

Name _____ Date _____

Intensive Pronouns

An intensive pronoun emphasizes a noun or another pronoun in a sentence, but can be dropped without changing the meaning of the sentence. Intensive pronouns always end in either **-self** or **-selves**. **Myself**, **yourself**, **himself**, **herself**, **itself**, **ourselves**, **yourselves**, and **themselves** are intensive pronouns.

He knows where the box is because he **himself** moved it.
After watching the movie, I wanted to read the book **itself**.

Circle the intensive pronoun in each sentence. Then underline the noun or pronoun to which the intensive pronoun refers.

1. I myself opened the jar.

2. You yourself agreed to bring donations for the food pantry.

3. The farmer himself cleaned the chicken coop.

4. We heard the updated information from the principal herself.

Write the correct intensive pronoun to complete each sentence.
Choose one of the following: *themselves*, *herself*, *itself*, *yourself*.

5. Roxy _____ created the masterpiece.

6. The hamster _____ knocked over its food dish.

7. The volunteers _____ weeded the entire community garden.

8. You _____ said that you wanted to go to a concert.

Intensive Pronouns

An intensive pronoun emphasizes a noun or another pronoun in a sentence, but can be dropped without changing the meaning of the sentence. Intensive pronouns always end in either **-self** or **-selves**. **Myself, yourself, himself, herself, itself, ourselves, yourselves,** and **themselves** are intensive pronouns.

Donna sent the <u>mayor</u> **himself** an invitation to the school play.
<u>I</u> **myself** stood in line to buy the tickets.

Write the correct intensive pronoun to complete each sentence. Choose one of the following: *Myself, yourself, himself, herself, itself, ourselves, yourselves, themselves.*

1. The choir members _____ haven't heard the good news yet.

2. We _____ liked the book even though it didn't get a good review.

3. The crowd cheered as the Olympian _____ waved to them.

4. You _____ agreed to mow the lawn.

5. My aunt _____ built the bunk beds.

6. Mr. Gupta invited the students _____ to teach tomorrow's lesson.

7. I _____ was surprised when my apple pie won first place.

8. Although the setting was quite plain, I loved the story _____.

9. The playground _____ was newly constructed.

10. Mia invited Luke _____ to the movie.

Name _____ Date _____

Intensive Pronouns

An intensive pronoun emphasizes a noun or another pronoun in a sentence, but can be dropped without changing the meaning of the sentence. Intensive pronouns always end in either **-self** or **-selves**. **Myself**, **yourself**, **himself**, **herself**, **itself**, **ourselves**, **yourselves**, and **themselves** are intensive pronouns.

You **yourselves** can make the posters for the book sale.

We **ourselves** can unpack all the books.

Write the correct intensive pronoun to complete each sentence. Choose one of the following: *Myself, yourself, himself, herself, itself, ourselves, yourselves, themselves*.

1. You _____ should ask the advisor about joining the debate team.

2. The friends _____ chose their new theme song.

3. We interviewed the lead actor _____ about his new play.

4. The chef _____ spoke to our club about her new cookbook.

5. I _____ would like to be a pilot someday.

6. We _____ made a project for the science fair.

7. The news channel ran a story about the school fair _____.

8. Brendan _____ painted his room a new color.

9. Mrs. Brant _____ should organize a class trip to the museum.

10. I _____ enjoyed looking at the photographs in the gallery.

11. The campers _____ marched through the woods to the lake.

12. Mary _____ went to pick up the supplies at the hardware store.

Pronoun-Antecedent Agreement

The noun that a pronoun replaces is called an antecedent. A pronoun and its antecedent must agree in number and person.

	Pronoun	Antecedent	Agreement
I put the book in **my** bag.	my	I	singular, first person
Sari, here are **your** test results.	your	Sari	singular, second person
The **students** wanted to help, so **they** organized a lake clean-up day.	they	students	plural, third person

Write the correct pronoun to complete each sentence. Choose one of the following: her, their, his, your, my, it, they.

1. Congress is the legislative branch, and _____ is in charge of making laws.

2. If people are equal under the law, _____ should have equal opportunities.

3. The teacher said Karana would have time later to revise _____ paper.

4. In an absolute monarchy, the queen or king is the supreme ruler, and her or _____ word is law.

5. The judges agree that _____ job is to interpret the law.

6. The director said, "Joy and Tyrell, it's time to rehearse _____ scene now."

7. Franklin stayed home and practiced _____ speech in preparation for class.

8. I am going to take _____ little sister to the lake for a swim.

Conquer Grammar • Grade 6 • © Newmark Learning, LLC

Pronoun-Antecedent Agreement

The noun that a pronoun replaces is called an antecedent. A pronoun and its antecedent must agree in number and person.

	Pronoun	Antecedent	Agreement
If **students** finish the test early, **they** can leave the room.	they	students	plural, third person
Wyatt is on the team because **he** can play well.	he	Wyatt	singular, third person

Circle the pronoun in the parentheses ( ) that correctly completes each sentence.

1. When my grandmother was younger, (you, they, she) had a typewriter.

2. I love going to the lake because (they, I, you) can relax all day.

3. If the two of us work together, (we, you, they) can finish cleaning today.

4. The team captains met with the principal, so (they, we, she) missed practice.

5. You can finish in an hour if (she, I, you) stay focused.

6. We took a video of the bird feeding (its, your, their) young.

7. The jazz band decided that (he, they, you) would perform next month.

8. The students study frequently so that (we, you, they) can get good grades.

9. I can buy milk when (she, I, you) go to the grocery store.

10. Jake had to go home because (he, you, they) needed to watch his brother.

11. The computer came with (she, its, we) own wireless mouse.

12. I can't go to the party because (your, they, I) have plans with Charlie.

Pronoun-Antecedent Agreement

The noun that a pronoun replaces is called an antecedent. A pronoun and its antecedent must agree in number and person.

	Pronoun	Antecedent	Agreement
Daria and Ted want to be in the race, so **they** will work out every day.	they	Daria and Ted	plural, third person

Circle the pronoun in the parentheses ( ) that correctly completes each sentence.

1. After the president took office, (himself, they, he) appointed a new secretary of state.

2. We realized (you, we, they) could carry the furniture if we worked together.

3. If you practice your violin regularly, (they, we, you) will get into the orchestra.

4. We are worried because (her, our, their) best drummers are graduating.

Circle the pronoun that is incorrect in each sentence. Then rewrite the sentence with the correct pronoun.

5. Evan and I will discuss the new club rules, so they will attend the meeting.

_____

6. The cheerleading squad chose the next routine they want to work on.

_____

7. Jing and Carla signed up for art classes so she could learn how to draw.

_____

Pronoun-Antecedent Agreement

The noun that a pronoun replaces is called an antecedent. A pronoun and its antecedent must agree in number and person.

	Pronoun	Antecedent	Agreement
Tom went to the store. **He** bought two apples.	he	Tom	singular, third person
If **students** don't understand an assignment, **they** should ask for help.	they	students	plural, third person

Circle the pronoun in the parentheses ( ) that correctly completes each sentence.

1. The sixth grade classes met earlier about (its, their, they) camping trip.

2. Nate and I brought (their, he, our) trail map and compass for the hike.

3. The coaches doubted (his, her, their) decision.

4. Ariel wrote a book report about (herself, she, her) favorite mystery.

5. You should proofread (yourself, your, you) report before you turn it in.

Circle the incorrect pronoun in each sentence. Then rewrite the sentence with the correct pronoun.

6. On its last walk, Dan made it to the park on time for the sunrise.

_____

7. Delia was late for work because her overslept.

_____

Name _____ Date _____

Pronoun-Antecedent Agreement

The noun that a pronoun replaces is called an antecedent. A pronoun and its antecedent must agree in number and person.

	Pronoun	Antecedent	Agreement
Wendy and Lin told Dad that **they** were going to the library.	they	Wendy and Lin	plural, third person
Mr. Ruiz announced **he** will give a test tomorrow.	he	Mr. Ruiz	singular, third person

Rewrite each sentence. Replace the underlined noun or noun phrase with the correct pronoun.

1. Noami said that <u>Noami</u> would be here soon.

_____

2. <u>The researchers</u> discovered some interesting documents.

_____

3. Julie and <u>Alberto</u> said the answer at the same time.

_____

4. Why did Marc water <u>the plant</u> twice a day?

_____

5. The special guest read a story to <u>the kindergarteners</u>.

_____

6. <u>Tianna and I</u> went swimming together.

_____

7. The director cast Gemma and <u>Carl</u> in the school play.

_____

Conquer Grammar • Grade 6 • © Newmark Learning, LLC

Pronoun-Antecedent Agreement

The noun that a pronoun replaces is called an antecedent. A pronoun and its antecedent must agree in number and person.

	Pronoun	Antecedent	Agreement
Tessa likes to jog. **She** ran five miles yesterday.	She	Tessa	singular, third person
I waited for **Gram and Gramps**. I was excited to see **them**.	them	Gram and Gramps	plural, third person

Rewrite each sentence. Replace the underlined noun or noun phrase with the correct pronoun.

1. Emilio bought decorations for his aquarium.

_____

2. Melanie likes to sing with her sisters.

_____

3. Charlotte went to the water polo match with her dad and Derek.

_____

4. The fans cheered and screamed for joy.

_____

5. The seals swam alongside the surfers.

_____

6. Uncle Anthony took Ricardo and me to the tournament.

_____

7. My friend and I went to a Renaissance fair.

_____

Vague Pronouns

A pronoun is vague when it's unclear which noun the pronoun refers to.
To correct a vague pronoun, replace the pronoun with its noun antecedent.

Vague: As soon as Belinda saw Hannah, she waved hello.

Corrected: As soon as **Belinda** saw Hannah, **Belinda** waved hello.
Belinda waved hello as soon as **she** saw Hannah.

Circle the sentence in which the antecedent is unclear.

1. a. Ollie's brother boasted that he won the competition.

   b. Ollie's brother boasted that Ollie won the competition.

2. a. I packed the fragile vases in bags, but the bags broke anyway.

   b. I packed the fragile vases in bags, but they broke anyway.

3. a. Jerome told his dad that his car had a flat tire.

   b. Jerome told his dad that his dad's car had a flat tire.

4. a. Mayra told Nicole that she had aced the test.

   b. Mayra said that Nicole had aced the test.

5. a. Christophe will let Tatsuo know if he can go to Simon's show.

   b. If Christophe can go to Simon's show, Christophe will let Tatsuo know.

6. a. Erika told Zoe that her holiday trip was in December.

   b. Erika told Zoe that Erika's holiday trip was in December.

Vague Pronouns

A pronoun is vague when it's unclear which noun the pronoun refers to.
To correct a vague pronoun, replace the pronoun with its noun antecedent.

Vague: Leo has a bike and scooter, but **it** broke.
Corrected: Leo has a bike and scooter, but **the bike** broke.
Leo has a bike and scooter, but **the scooter** broke.

In each sentence, circle the vague pronoun. Underline the two possible noun antecedents.

1. The cat chased the dog away from its favorite place on the couch.

2. Zac told Dad his shirt had a hole in it.

3. Dad drove Eric to the game after he watered the vegetable garden.

4. Maria bought a t-shirt and a dress, but it was too big for her.

Rewrite each sentence twice. Replace the vague pronoun with both possible noun antecedents.

5. I was putting my flute in the case, and I dropped it.

a._____

b._____

6. Lia borrowed my binoculars and compass, but she forgot to return it.

a._____

b._____

Vague Pronouns

A pronoun is vague when it's unclear which noun the pronoun refers to.
To correct a vague pronoun, replace the pronoun with its noun antecedent.

Vague: Felix told Carey that it's **his** turn to hit the ball.
Corrected: Felix told Carey that it's **Felix's** turn to hit the ball.
Felix told Carey that it's **Carey's** turn to hit the ball.

Circle the vague pronoun or pronouns in each sentence. Then underline the two possible noun antecedents.

1. Andrea has a tablet and a cell phone, but she left it at home.

2. Ted ran into Roy when he left the theater.

3. Kim boarded the bus with Mariana after she left the office.

4. Greg told his brother that he was running too fast.

5. Amy was walking with Julia when she found a five-dollar bill.

Rewrite each sentence twice. Replace the vague pronoun with both possible noun antecedents.

6. When Yolanda forgot to return Marisol's blue sweater, she was upset.

a. _____

b. _____

7. Rahim and Sean high-fived when he scored the winning goal.

a. _____

b. _____

Name _____ Date _____

Vague Pronouns

A pronoun is vague when it's unclear which noun the pronoun refers to.
To correct a vague pronoun, replace the pronoun with its noun antecedent.

Vague: Will and Alex invited their friends to the game, but **they** got lost on the way to the stadium.

Corrected: Will and Alex invited their friends to the game, but **their friends** got lost on the way to the stadium.

Will and Alex invited their friends to the game, but **Will and Alex** got lost on the way to the stadium.

Circle the vague pronoun in each sentence. Then rewrite the sentence twice. Replace the vague pronoun with both possible noun antecedents.

1. Alba asked Raquel for help on a project after she finished her own assignment.

a. _____

b. _____

2. As Austin added flour to the mixing bowl, he knocked it over.

a. _____

b. _____

3. Take the jewelry box out of the cabinet and lock it.

a. _____

b. _____

4. My dad called Terrence after he lost his wallet.

a. _____

b. _____

Adjectives

Adjectives are words that describe nouns. Follow this order when using more than one adjective to describe a noun: number (**three**, **many**), opinion (**boring**, **interesting**), size (**tiny**, **enormous**), looks/feels (**hot**, **slimy**), age (**young**, **ancient**), shape (**jagged**, **round**) color (**red**, **striped**), origin (**American**, **Greek**), material (**nylon**, **wool**). Place a comma after each adjective, except a number and between the last adjective and the noun.

> **Incorrect:** I have **two, fluffy, lovable, small,** dogs.
> **Correct:** I have **two lovable, small, fluffy** dogs.

Circle the adjectives that are in the correct order. Write the adjectives on the line with correct punctuation.

1. Mom always takes her _____ briefcase to the office.

    a. sleek brown leather   **b.** leather brown sleek

2. Our granny still refers to us as her _____ babies.

    a. sweet little two   **b.** two sweet little

3. He finished fifth after _____ marathon runners.

    a. four Kenyan muscular fast   **b.** four fast muscular Kenyan

4. How much _____ pie do you want?

    a. delicious juicy berry   **b.** juicy berry delicious

5. We are stuck on this _____ airplane.

    a. boring packed stuffy   **b.** boring stuffy packed

6. Tourists visit the _____ ruins.

    a. stone crumbling ancient   **b.** ancient crumbling stone

Adjectives

Adjectives are words that describe nouns. Follow this order when using more than one adjective to describe a noun: number (**thirty**, **some**), opinion (**clever**, **scary**), size (**small**, **massive**), looks/feels (**plump**, **rough**), age (**young**, **modern**), shape (**square**, **triangular**), color (**pastel**, **brick red**), origin (**Chinese**, **Peruvian**), material (**plastic**, **concrete**). Place a comma after each adjective, except a number and between the last adjective and the noun.

> **Incorrect:** My dog Jericho buried **two, new, meaty, large,** bones.
> **Correct:** My dog Jericho buried **two new, large, meaty** bones.

Write the adjectives on the line in the correct order with proper punctuation.

1. The horse ate _____ carrots.

(long   orange   three   fresh)

2. We hosted a _____ exchange student.

(15-year-old   tall   Swedish   kind)

3. I placed _____ vases on a shelf in the closet.

(fragile   small   antique   several)

4. Our neighbors hung _____wind chimes on their porch.

(four   wooden   new   different-sized)

5. Luckily, I have _____ companions.

(local   many   11-year-old   friendly)

6. My parents attended a _____ performance.

(musical   2-hour-long   funny)

Comparative Adjectives

The comparative form of an adjective is used to compare two nouns. Follow these spelling rules to form comparative adjectives: Add **-er** to the end of an adjective to make it comparative. For adjectives that end in an **e**, add **-r**. For some adjectives that end in **y** change the **y** to **i** and then add **-er**. For some one-syllable adjectives, double the last consonant and add **-er**. If the adjective has three or more syllables, form the comparative by placing the word **more** in front of the adjective.

Adjective	Comparative Form
old	older
nice	nicer
scary	scarier
red	redder
beautiful	more beautiful

Circle the correct comparative adjective in the parentheses ( ). Then write the complete sentence on the line.

1. The cartoon before the film was actually (funnier, funnyer) than the movie itself.

   _____

2. The cruise ship is (bigier, bigger) than the sailboat.

   _____

3. These trees are (greener, more green) than those shrubs.

   _____

4. Thanks to her vivid imagery, this novel is (incredibler, more incredible) than her last one.

   _____

5. Our young doctor was (capabler, more capable) and (wiseer, wiser) than we first thought.

   _____

Conquer Grammar • Grade 6 • © Newmark Learning, LLC

Superlative Adjectives

The superlative form of an adjective is used to compare three or more nouns. Follow these spelling rules to form superlative adjectives: Add **-est** to the end of an adjective to make it superlative. For adjectives that end in **e**, simply add **-st**. For some adjectives that end in **y** change the **y** to **i** and then add **-est**. For some one-syllable adjectives, double the last consonant and add **-est**. If the adjective has three or more syllables, form the comparative by placing the word **most** in front of the adjective.

Adjective	Superlative Form
old	oldest
nice	nicest
scary	scariest
red	reddest
beautiful	most beautiful

Complete each sentence with the superlative form of the adjective in the parentheses ( ).

1. Do you know which climate is the _____?

(dry)

2. The Hodges family live the _____ to our house.

(close)

3. I cried because it was the _____ movie I've ever seen.

(sad)

4. My parents threw the _____ party when my brother graduated

from college. (fancy)

5. Study hard, because this is the _____ test we'll take all year!

(important)

6. Mia has the _____ hair out of all the girls on the soccer team.

(curly)

Adverbs

An adverb gives more information about where or when an action occurs or how it happens. An adverb can appear before or after the verb it modifies or in between different verb parts. Adverbs can also modify an adjective or another adverb. In those cases, the adverb should appear before the word it modifies.

Modifies a verb: Yesterday, our cat stalked her toy mouse.
Modifies an adjective: She is an **extremely** talented singer.
Modifies an adverb: The tiger pounced **quite** forcefully.

Circle the adverb in each sentence. Underline the word it modifies and write whether the word is a verb, adjective, or adverb.

1. The amusement park will reopen soon for the summer season. _____

2. I eagerly anticipate my first ride on the The Mariner. _____

3. This town is named perfectly, due to its proximity to the sea. _____

4. In my mind, I can hear the very loud screams during the first drop. _____

5. The cars hold two people and we are strapped in quite well. _____

6. When the ride ends, the screams turn instantly to laughter. _____

7. The rabbit hopped quickly into the bushes. _____

8. The ticket was really expensive. _____

Relative Adverbs

A relative adverb introduces a relative clause and refers to a time, a place, or a reason. The relative clause gives more information about a word or phrase in the sentence. The words **when**, **where**, and **why** may be used as relative adverbs.

Time: March is **when** <u>the daffodils bloom</u>.
Place: California is **where** <u>we once lived</u>.
Reason: I know the reason **why** <u>the dogs were barking</u>.

Underline the relative clause in each sentence. Circle the relative adverb.

1. Wednesday is when I have my singing lesson.

2. Southern France is where lavender grows well.

3. I'll always remember the day when I learned to ride a bicycle.

4. Our train conductor explained the reason why the train was delayed.

5. I arrived at the Grand Canyon, where I have been wanting to hike.

6. He did not understand the reason why his parents were frustrated.

7. Ethan quickly learned why the trail was so difficult.

8. Tomorrow is when I hear about my test score.

Comparative Adverbs

The comparative form of an adverb is used to compare two things. For most adverbs that end in **ly**, form the comparative by placing the word **more** in front of the adverb. Add **-er** to the end of almost all other regular adverbs to form the comparative.

Adverb	Comparative Form
loudly	more loudly
hard	harder
late	later

Circle the correct comparative adverb in the parentheses ( ) to complete each sentence. Then rewrite each sentence.

1. The books were arranged (neatlier, more neatly) than the art supplies.

   _____

2. We are (nearer, more near) our home than we were an hour ago.

   _____

3. This ice cream tastes (sweeter, more sweet) than the first flavor.

   _____

4. The special day arrived (sooner, more soon) than I imagined.

   _____

5. Why is my sister now doing her chores (happilier, more happily) than last week?

   _____

6. The rain fell (softlier, more softly) than the hail.

   _____

Conquer Grammar • Grade 6 • © Newmark Learning, LLC

Superlative Adverbs

The superlative form of an adverb is used to compare three or more things.
For most adverbs that end in **ly**, form the comparative by placing the word **most**
in front of the adverb. Add **-est** to the end of almost all other regular adverbs to form
the superlative.

Adverb	Superlative Form
loudly	most loudly
hard	hardest
late	latest

**Complete each sentence with the superlative form of the adverb
in the parentheses ( ).**

1. The sun shines the _____ of all the stars in the sky.

                    (brightly)

2. Six o'clock in the evening is the _____ I can be home for dinner.

                    (soon)

3. Who is the _____ swimmer on the team?

                    (fast)

4. We all agree that my sister sings the _____.

                    (sweetly)

5. Miss Ford is the _____ of all the teachers at our school.

                    (kind)

6. I see the _____ when I wear my eyeglasses.

                    (clearly)

7. Today was the _____ day of the year.

                    (cold)

Prepositions

A preposition shows the relationship between a noun or pronoun and another word in the sentence. The relationship may show **what, when, where,** or **how.** Some common prepositions include **about, above, across, after, against, around, at, before, behind, below, beside, between, by, during, for, from, in, near, of, on, out, over, through, to, toward, under, until, up, with.**

We sat **under** <u>a shady tree</u> and listened **to** <u>music</u> **for** <u>an hour</u>.
My service dog came **with** <u>us</u>.

Circle each preposition and underline the noun or noun phrase that relates to the preposition.

1. Luckily, my favorite park is near my house.

2. You can see many colorful birds in the trees.

3. Someday, I want to row a boat across the lake.

4. I often ride my bicycle around the perimeter.

5. There will be many concerts at the stadium.

6. We try to go with our friends when we can.

7. There are fireflies glowing by the bushes.

8. The dogs sat under the table.

9. Put your umbrella beside the door.

10. My sister and I walked toward the lake.

Conquer Grammar • Grade 6 • © Newmark Learning, LLC

Prepositions

A preposition shows the relationship between a noun or pronoun and another word in the sentence. The relationship may show **what**, **when**, **where**, or **how**. Some common prepositions include **about, above, across, after, against, around, at, before, behind, below, beside, between, by, during, for, from, in, near, of, on, out, over, through, to, toward, under, until, up, with**.

The boys ran **through** <u>the narrow hallway</u>.

Write a preposition or prepositions to complete each sentence.

1. The ferry took us _____ the island.

2. We traveled _____ the ocean's choppy water.

3. The journey took _____ twenty and twenty-five minutes.

4. I forgot to check my watch _____ we left the shore.

5. We walked _____ the dock _____ the town.

6. After wandering _____ charming streets, we found a place _____ rest.

7. _____ our brief visit, we only got an overview _____ this lovely place.

8. The kitten hid _____ the boxes.

Correlative Conjunctions

Correlative conjunctions always come in pairs and appear in different parts of a sentence. They work together to connect the parts of the sentence.
Use the correlative conjunctions **both** . . . **and** to add one idea to another.
Either . . . **or** gives an alternative. **Neither** . . . **nor** gives no alternative.
Not only . . . **but also** contrasts two ideas.

Both Michelle **and** Bonnie want to learn a new language.
They will choose **either** Spanish **or** French.
Neither Italian **nor** German is offered at their school.
Learning another language is **not only** challenging **but also** rewarding.

Join each pair of sentences with the correlative conjunctions in the parentheses ( ). Write the sentence on the line.

1. At the farm, there was an apple orchard. There was also a pumpkin patch.

   (both . . . and)

   _____

2. We can buy an apple pie. We can buy a pumpkin pie.

   (either . . . or)

   _____

3. Ice cream is good on pie. Whipped cream is tasty on it, too.

   (not only . . . but also)

   _____

4. The pumpkin was too heavy. My brother and I couldn't lift it.

   (neither . . . nor)

   _____

5. My brother wants to be a farmer. So do I.

   (both . . . and)

   _____

Nonrestrictive Clauses

Nonrestrictive clauses are not essential to the meaning of a sentence. A nonrestrictive clause can be deleted without changing the sentence's meaning. Nonrestrictive clauses are usually set off from the rest of the sentence with commas, dashes, or parentheses.

The novels**, which are my favorites,** are now movies, too.

The novels **(which are my favorites)** are now movies, too.

The novels**—which are my favorites—**are now movies, too.

Rewrite each sentence. Use the punctuation named in the parentheses ( ) to set off the nonrestrictive clause.

1. Alonzo who is a little shy isn't sure he wants to audition for the play. (commas)

_____

2. I hope though I am doubtful that he'll change his mind. (parentheses)

_____

3. Dory and Ray both terrific artists are working on the scenery. (dashes)

_____

4. Josh who is very funny is writing a comedy sketch. (commas)

_____

5. The materials which I still need to buy are on sale. (commas)

_____

6. My aunt who sews her own clothes will help with the costumes. (dashes)

_____

Nonrestrictive Clauses

Nonrestrictive clauses are not essential to the meaning of a sentence. A nonrestrictive clause can be deleted without changing the sentence's meaning. Nonrestrictive clauses are usually set off from the rest of the sentence with commas, dashes, or parentheses.

Curtis, **who won the blue ribbon for his illustration,** is my cousin.

Two of my classmates **(Val and Chiara)** made the team.

The Lightning Thief—**the best book ever!**—is about twelve-year-old Percy Jackson.

Rewrite each sentence. Use the punctuation named in the parentheses ( ) to set off the nonrestrictive clause.

1. T.J. the boy who aced the geometry test is my brother. (parentheses)

_____

2. We Shelli and Kiara raced to the finish line. (dashes)

_____

3. My mother who is a police officer is going to speak about safety. (commas)

_____

4. My bicycle which is in the garage needs new brakes. (parentheses)

_____

5. A great song my favorite one in the whole world! just came on the radio. (dashes)

_____

6. Ricky who is the smartest boy I know wants to be a professor someday. (commas)

_____

Nonrestrictive Clauses

Nonrestrictive clauses are not essential to the meaning of a sentence. A nonrestrictive clause can be deleted without changing the sentence's meaning. Nonrestrictive clauses are usually set off from the rest of the sentence with commas, dashes, or parentheses.

Cole**, who sits next to me in Spanish class,** is my best friend.
Both of my favorite teams **(San Antonio and Cleveland)** are in the finals!
*Holes***—my favorite book—**was made into a movie.

Rewrite each sentence. Use the punctuation named in the parentheses ( ) to set off the nonrestrictive clause.

1. Kendall who is class president is absent today. (commas)

_____

2. Lulu wants to visit all three cities London, Rome, and Shanghai. (parentheses)

_____

3. The toddlers who are really energetic ran around in the yard. (dashes)

_____

4. We Paco, Jessie, and I decided to go to the library today. (parentheses)

_____

5. Three students Aldo, Ricky, and Jen volunteered to help. (dashes)

_____

6. I painted my bike red my favorite color, but it's not dry yet. (parentheses)

_____

7. I like to eat grapes sour or sweet with cheese. (parentheses)

_____

Nonrestrictive Clauses

Nonrestrictive clauses are not essential to the meaning of a sentence. A nonrestrictive clause can be deleted without changing the sentence's meaning. Nonrestrictive clauses are usually set off from the rest of the sentence with commas, dashes, or parentheses.

Mr. Green, **who lives next door,** works at the art supply store.

Rewrite each sentence. Use the punctuation named in the parentheses ( ) to set off the nonrestrictive clause.

1. Victoria asked Carly who's in her class if she could borrow a pencil.   (commas)

   _____

2. The two friends Tory and Sarah Jane are writing a song.   (parentheses)

   _____

3. That shot Malcolm made that last one was incredible!   (dashes)

   _____

4. The note which was written in code told me where to go.   (commas)

   _____

5. Mara who is my best friend lives in Oregon.   (parentheses)

   _____

6. To train for the race which I want to win I cycle five miles a day.   (commas)

   _____

7. Ralph found all of Ariel's e-mail addresses two in total in the directory. (dashes)

   _____

Nonrestrictive and Restrictive Clauses

A nonrestrictive clause is not essential to a sentence's meaning. Nonrestrictive clauses are usually set off from the rest of the sentence with commas, dashes, or parentheses.

My neighbor, **whom I admire,** is a veterinarian.
My neighbor **(whom I admire)** is a veterinarian.
My neighbor—**whom I admire**—is a veterinarian.

A restrictive clause is essential to a sentence's meaning, and should not be set off from the rest of the sentence.

The genre **that I like best** is science fiction.

If the underlined clause is restrictive, write _R_. If it is nonrestrictive, write _N_ and add commas where needed.

1. Our school will be closed on Thanksgiving <u>which is my favorite holiday</u>. _____

2. Sanjay loves any book <u>that is about Greek or Roman mythology</u>. _____

3. The actor <u>who is in my favorite movie</u> will be at the mall on Saturday. _____

4. Jeremiah <u>the boy we met last week</u> will be at the pool party. _____

Rewrite each sentence. Use the punctuation named in the parentheses ( ) to set off the nonrestrictive clause.

5. North Street as seen on the map is near Fairview Avenue. (parentheses)

_____

6. The tuba I know it's big is the instrument I'm learning to play. (dashes)

_____

7. The glee club which rehearses daily will perform on Friday. (commas)

_____

Name _____ Date _____

Nonrestrictive and Restrictive Clauses

A nonrestrictive clause is not essential to a sentence's meaning. Nonrestrictive clauses are usually set off from the rest of the sentence with commas, dashes, or parentheses.

The director, **who is our mentor,** thought the actors were great.

A restrictive clause is essential to a sentence's meaning, and should not be set off from the rest of the sentence.

The actors **who attended every rehearsal** knew their lines.

If the underlined clause is restrictive, write _R_. If it is nonrestrictive, write _N_ and add commas where needed.

1. My favorite state <u>which is where I learned to surf</u> is Hawaii. _____

2. The dog <u>that lives next door</u> digs many holes under our fence. _____

3. The boy <u>who broke the vase</u> offered to pay for the repair. _____

Rewrite each sentence. Use the punctuation named in the parentheses ( ) to set off the nonrestrictive clause.

4. Lavonne who is my best friend wants to be a marine biologist. (commas)

_____

5. Riley's performance which we're both going to is tomorrow. (parentheses)

_____

6. My chair which is really cozy is my dog's favorite place to nap. (dashes)

_____

Nonrestrictive and Restrictive Clauses

A nonrestrictive clause is not essential to a sentence's meaning. Nonrestrictive clauses are usually set off from the rest of the sentence with commas, dashes, or parentheses.

Hamir and Max, **who are teammates,** are good basketball players.

A restrictive clause is essential to a sentence's meaning, and should not be set off from the rest of the sentence.

The van **that is parked out in front** is my aunt's.

If the underlined clause is restrictive, write _R_. If it is nonrestrictive, write _N_ and rewrite the sentence with correct punctuation.

1. The sculpture <u>that is in the dining room</u> is very expensive.

_____

2. I handed in my short story <u>which is about an adventure in the desert</u>.

_____

3. Romy's favorite city <u>which is also mine</u> is New Orleans.

_____

4. Armand offers tutoring for students <u>who are struggling in algebra</u>.

_____

5. Mary's drum set <u>which her sister gave her</u> is bright red.

_____

6. Mr. Rossi <u>who is my neighbor</u> is a terrific saxophone player.

_____

7. The house <u>that is on the corner of the street</u> has a stone facade.

_____

Punctuation for Effect

Use an exclamation point (**!**) to add excitement or tension to a sentence that shows strong feeling. An ellipsis (**...**) can signal a pause or shift in thinking.

Stop that right now**!**
Well, now**...**I'm just not sure about this.

Rewrite each sentence. Add an exclamation point where it would be most effective.

1. Wow. That woman is an amazing athlete.

_____

2. Good grief. Did you hear that?

_____

3. I'm competing in my first race tomorrow. I'm very nervous.

_____

Rewrite each sentence. Use an ellipsis for effect.

4. Hmmm I don't think I'll try that casserole.

_____

5. If I don't get a part in the play better not to dwell on it.

_____

6. If that happens I guess it doesn't matter.

_____

Punctuation for Effect

Use an exclamation point (**!**) to add excitement or tension to a sentence that shows strong feeling. An ellipsis (**...**) can signal a pause or shift in thinking.

No way**!** I'm not any good at acting**...**or maybe I am.

Rewrite each sentence. Add an exclamation point or an ellipsis where it would be most effective.

1. It started to snow after the first inning. I just couldn't believe it.

_____

2. I'm staying home, and that's final.

_____

3. I'd like to go. I'm just concerned that I won't know anyone there.

_____

4. Well I wish you'd reconsider.

_____

5. I turned the corner and saw it. A turkey stood right on Oak Lane.

_____

6. Oh, no. I've lost my library book.

_____

7. We wonder what would have occurred. Oh well, we'll never know now.

_____

Capitalization in Dialogue

Dialogue is a conversation between two or more people or characters. Quotation marks set off a speaker's exact words. Always capitalize the first word in the quotation marks. If the dialogue is interrupted, do not capitalize the first word in the continuation of the dialogue unless the speaker's tag ends in a period.

"**L**et's meet at my house today," said my best friend.
Peter said, "**Y**ou have a dentist appointment tomorrow."
"**L**et's meet at my house," Lucy said, "**s**o we can walk to the station."

Rewrite each sentence with correct capitalization.

1. Mr. Peterson announced, "your research papers were all very impressive."

_____

2. "what are your plans for the weekend?" asked Irma.

_____

3. "my plans involve studying," I said. "they will also include basketball."

_____

4. Irma inquired, "would you like to shoot some hoops with my brother and me?"

_____

5. "sure, but could we meet on Sunday?" I answered.

_____

6. "if I get all my work done on Saturday, I'll have much more fun," I promised.

_____

7. "so, Sunday it is," said Irma, "And we can meet at my house."

_____

Capitalization and Punctuation in Titles

Capitalize the first and last word and each additional main word of a book or song title. Unless it is the first or last word of the title, do not capitalize **a**, **an**, and **the**, or most short prepositions, such as **at**, **in**, **by**, **for**, **of**, and **to**. Always underline a book, movie, or magazine title and place an article, poem, song, or story title in quotation marks.

Book title: <u>A Wrinkle in Time</u>
Song title: "America the Beautiful"

Rewrite each sentence with correct capitalization. Be sure to underline the book titles and put quotation marks around the song titles.

1. I am reading the book, math and music, to find out how the topics are similar.

_____

2. I liked reading little women, but my brother preferred the call of the wild.

_____

3. The patriotic song, you're a grand old flag, is very catchy.

_____

4. I just finished reading about a vet in the book, all creatures great and small.

_____

5. The first song I can remember singing is twinkle, twinkle, little star.

_____

6. My father's favorite mystery novel is the hound of the baskervilles.

_____

Capitalization and Punctuation in Titles

Capitalize the first and last word and each additional main word of a book or song title. Unless it is the first or last word of the title, do not capitalize **a**, **an**, and **the**, or most short prepositions, such as **at**, **in**, **by**, **for**, **of**, and **to**. Always underline a book, movie, play, or magazine title and place an article, poem, song, or story title in quotation marks.

Book title: The Odyssey
Article title: "The Scientist"

Underline the title in each sentence. Then rewrite the sentence with correct punctuation and capitalization.

1. I borrowed a copy of national geographic from the magazine rack.

_____

2. Have you seen the movie where the red fern grows, based on the book?

_____

3. My parents read the new york times every Sunday.

_____

4. Shakespeare's romeo and juliet is a play most people are familiar with.

_____

5. I bought biking around paris to take on our trip.

_____

6. My sister loved the classic movie she saw last weekend, the sound of music.

_____

Capitalization and Punctuation in Titles

Capitalize the first and last word and each additional main word of a book or song title. Unless it is the first or last word of the title, do not capitalize **a**, **an**, and **the**, or most short prepositions, such as **at**, **in**, **by**, **for**, **of**, and **to**. Always underline a book, movie, or magazine title and place an article, poem, song, or story title in quotation marks.

Rewrite each sentence with correct capitalization and punctuation for the titles.

1. I just finished a great article, the secret world of icebergs.

_____

2. I am trying to memorize paul revere's ride, a poem by

Henry Wadsworth Longfellow.

_____

_____

3. I liked Poe's short story, the black cat, but my brother preferred

the tell-tale heart.

_____

_____

4. May I teach you the song I learned at summer camp, on top of spaghetti?

_____

5. My mother's favorite short story is the legend of sleepy hollow.

_____

Sentence Fragments

A sentence fragment is an incomplete sentence that does not express a complete thought. It is missing a subject, a verb, or both. To correct a fragment, add the missing subject or verb.

Fragment: Ran the race in record time.

Complete sentence: Lizzy ran the race in record time.

Fragment: The crowd for her achievement.

Complete sentence: The crowd **cheered** for her achievement.

Determine which of the two choices is a fragment and which is a complete sentence. Circle the fragment.

1. **a.** The community center across the road from the school.

   b. The community center is right across the road from the school.

2. **a.** The two girls studied for their history test next week.

   b. Studied for the history test next week.

3. **a.** We should have enough games and activities for the party at Rivington Park.

   b. Enough games and activities for the party at Rivington Park.

Rewrite each fragment as a complete sentence. Circle the word in the parentheses ( ) that corrects the fragment. Then write the complete sentence on the line.

4. The team to the field after the rain delay.   (players, returned)

   _____

5. The announced that a prize had been awarded.   (judge, earlier)

   _____

6. The badminton players in the gym.   (coach, practiced)

   _____

Run-On Sentences

A run-on sentence contains two or more complete thoughts. One way to correct a run-on sentence is to separate it into two or more complete sentences, each with a subject and a verb. Another way is to add a comma between the complete thoughts and a coordinating conjunction such as **and**, **but**, **or**, or **so**.

> **Run-On:** April went to the store after school she bought a yogurt.
> **Corrected:** April went to the store after school. **S**he bought a yogurt.
> April went to the store after school, **and** she bought a yogurt.

Rewrite each run-on sentence as two or more complete sentences.

1. Did Dawn research whales online did she find enough information?

_____

2. If she likes animals, she should study zoology she should study biology, too.

_____

3. Marianne was absent for three days she is behind in her group project.

_____

4. I can't believe that he didn't hear the thunder it was so loud!

_____

5. Have you finished I think it's finally my turn.

_____

6. I can't believe it that is an amazing story!

_____

7. We went for a walk in the woods and saw some unusual birds, which I loved, then we went to get lunch, which I thought was pretty tasty, it was a delightful day.

_____

_____

Run-On Sentences

A run-on sentence contains two or more complete thoughts. One way to correct a run-on sentence is to separate it into two or more complete sentences, each with a subject and a verb. Another way is to add a comma between the complete thoughts and a coordinating conjunction such as **and**, **but**, **or**, or **so**.

> **Run-On:** My father knew I was exhausted he let me sleep.
> **Corrected:** My father knew I was exhausted. **H**e let me sleep.
> My father knew I was exhausted, **so** he let me sleep.

Correct each run-on sentence. Use a comma and the conjunction in the parentheses ( ). Write the new sentence on the line.

1. Jada is on the track team Christa is on the volleyball team.　(and)

_____

2. Cesar likes algebra Jean-Pierre prefers language arts.　(but)

_____

3. Serena placed first in the state she is going to the nationals.　(so)

_____

4. We could order sushi for lunch we could get pizza.　(or)

_____

5. Eli wanted to ride the roller coaster he's too little.　(but)

_____

6. I want to ace the next exam I'm going to study for an hour every night.　(so)

_____

7. Lucas went to a movie in the morning he saw a play in the evening.　(and)

_____

Run-On Sentences

A run-on sentence contains two or more complete thoughts. One way to correct a run-on sentence is to separate it into two or more complete sentences, each with a subject and a verb. Another way is to add a comma between the complete thoughts and a coordinating conjunction such as **and**, **but**, **or**, or **so**.

Run-On: We've had so much rain they say it's good for the plants.

Corrected: We've had so much rain. **T**hey say it's good for the plants.

We've had so much rain, **but** they say it's good for the plants.

Rewrite each run-on sentence as two complete sentences.

1. It is nearly four o'clock the ferry will already have left.

_____

2. Marguerite practices her piccolo every day she adores music.

_____

3. Have you finished reading that chapter yet can you go outside now?

_____

Correct each run-on sentence. Use a comma and the conjunction in the parentheses ( ). Write the new sentence on the line.

4. Kenneth is my brother Kenny is his nickname.   (and)

_____

5. It's Sunday the library is closed.   (so)

_____

6. Carter loved the movie Rafael preferred the book.   (but)

_____

Sentence Fragments and Run-On Sentences

A sentence fragment does not express a complete thought. It is missing a subject, a verb, or both. To correct a fragment, add the missing subject or verb. A run-on sentence consists of two or more complete thoughts. One way to correct a run-on sentence is to divide it into two or more complete sentences. Another way is to add a comma between the complete thoughts and a coordinating conjunction such as **and**, **but**, **or**, or **so**.

Fragment: Runs with her dog whenever the weather is nice.
Corrected: Yolanda runs with her dog whenever the weather is nice.

Run-On: Harry brought an extra bottle of juice he was sure he'd be thirsty.
Corrected: Harry brought an extra bottle of juice. **H**e was sure he'd be thirsty.

Rewrite each run-on sentence as two complete sentences.

1. The queen appointed the ministers they were her most trusted advisors.

_____

2. Anna was a respected queen she reigned for decades.

_____

3. We saw the coronation on TV it was spectacular!

_____

Circle the word or phrase in the parentheses ( ) that corrects the fragment. Then write each fragment as a complete sentence.

4. Voted for the bill.   (The ministers, Last week)

_____

5. As the ball sailed through the goalpost!   (The crowd, Fans cheered)

_____

6. Studying for the spelling quiz?   (Are you, Why)

_____

Name _____ Date _____

Complex Sentences

A complex sentence consists of an independent clause joined with a dependent clause by a subordinate conjunction. Subordinate conjunctions include **although**, **since**, **because**, **until**, **while**, **that**, **when**, and **where**. If the conjunction begins the sentence, place a comma between the clauses.

I kept reading the short story **until** I finished it.
Although I have practiced steadily, I am not yet ready for the piano recital.

Draw one line under the independent clause in each sentence.
Draw two lines under the dependent clause.

1. The little girl laughed because her big brother made a funny face.

2. When our alarm didn't go off, my sister and I overslept.

3. The birds soared above the lake while the giraffes drank from it.

4. Although the day was hot, there was a refreshing breeze.

Combine each pair of sentences to form a complex sentence. Use a subordinate conjunction and a comma if needed. Write the sentence on the line.

5. Honey bees are considered social insects. They work together for survival.

_____

6. These bees live in a hive. They are very industrious.

_____

Name _____ Date _____

Complex Sentences

A complex sentence consists of an independent clause joined with a dependent clause by a subordinate conjunction. Subordinate conjunctions include **although**, **since**, **because**, **until**, **while**, **that**, **when**, and **where**. If the conjunction begins the sentence, place a comma between the clauses.

I had to go the store **since** I decided to cook the soup.
Although I have practiced steadily**,** I am not quite ready to perform the play.

Combine the two sentences to form a complex sentence. Use a subordinate conjunction and a comma if needed. Write the sentence on the line.

1. The amusement park may reopen soon. The weather still isn't quite warm enough.

_____

2. I had on my rain boots. I freely stepped into the deep puddle.

_____

3. We walked close to the fragile artwork. One of the museum guards reminded us to be careful.

_____

_____

4. I want to be famous someday. My success will probably follow many years of hard work.

_____

_____

5. The wind was blowing very hard today. We flew the kites.

_____

Reducing Sentences

Writers often reduce sentences by deleting words and phrases that are unnecessary or not important. Reducing sentences helps make writing clearer.

To relax, we listened to some soothing music ~~but I'm not sure who the artist is~~.

When I was 7 years old ~~or maybe 7 and a half~~, I lost my first tooth.

Rewrite each sentence. Delete any unnecessary or unimportant information.

1. My teacher, who is named Mrs. Greene just like my neighbor, read a wonderful story to the class.

_____

2. The new song I just heard on the radio that sounded like another song whose name I can't remember is really upbeat.

_____

3. Whenever it's time to harvest my vegetable garden, I'm surprised to see how much the deer have eaten, and I see those deer all around my neighborhood.

_____

_____

4. I liked how fresh the grass smelled in the foggy morning air, even though some of the grass was green and some of it was brown.

_____

5. I saw Mr. Hodge's car window was open and I heard emergency warnings going off because a dangerous storm was about to hit our town.

_____

_____

Varying Sentence Patterns

Skilled writers use a variety of sentence types to create interest and avoid choppy writing. One way to vary sentences is by combining related sentences using a comma and a conjunction such as **and**, **but**, **or**, **so**, or **yet**.

Steph bought a watch**, and** I did, too.
Angie bought a vest**, but** she didn't get anything else.
Amir can buy a new tie**, or** he can borrow his dad's.
Myra bought mittens**, so** her hands are no longer cold.
Yoshi liked the jacket**, yet** he chose not to buy it.

Rewrite each pair of sentences as one complete sentence. Use a comma and the conjunction in the parentheses ( ).

1. Ebony swam across the pool. Her brother timed her.   (and)

_____

2. The boys complained about the drizzle. They continued to play soccer.   (yet)

_____

3. My sister is right-handed. I am left-handed.   (but)

_____

4. We could see a ballet. We could go to the opera.   (or)

_____

5. The mail carrier crossed the street. She avoided the barking dog.   (so)

_____

6. Bella ate an orange. I ate a bowl of cherries.   (and)

_____

7. Lana entered the store. She bought shoes.   (and)

_____

Conquer Grammar • Grade 6 • © Newmark Learning, LLC

Name _____ Date _____

Varying Sentence Patterns

Skilled writers use a variety of sentence types to create interest and avoid choppy writing. One way to vary sentences is by combining related sentences using a comma and a conjunction such as **and**, **but**, **or**, **so**, or **yet**. You may also use the conjunction **and** or **or** to join the subjects (if the predicate appears in both sentences) or predicates (if the subject appears in both sentences) of two sentences.

Jasmine walked to the store, **but** it was closed.
Jasmine **and** Frida walked to the store.

Rewrite each sentence. Use a conjunction to combine the two sentences. Be sure to add a comma if needed.

1. Last weekend, my mom and I went to our neighbor's house. Mom and I went to see her new puppies.

_____

_____

2. My mom let me pick out a puppy. I took her home.

_____

3. We bought some toys for the new puppy. We set up a dog bed, too.

_____

4. I got the puppy yesterday. She can't stop wagging her tail.

_____

5. My friend Roberto likes to snowboard. I like to snowboard, too.

_____

6. The snow is cold. Our special gear keeps us warm.

_____

Name _____ Date _____

Varying Sentence Patterns

There are several ways to vary sentence patterns. You can combine related sentences with a conjunction such as **after**, **although**, **because**, **before**, **if**, **since**, **when**, **while**, or **unless**. You can also switch the order of the words in a sentence, beginning the sentence with a conjunction. Always place a comma after the phrase introduced by the conjunction.

I studied hard **because** I wanted to do well in school.
Because I wanted to do well in school**,** I studied hard.

Rewrite each paragraph. Combine sentences and begin sentences with one of the following conjunctions: after, although, because, before, if, since, when, while, unless.

1. The Grand Canyon attracts millions of visitors each year. It is considered one of the seven natural wonders of the world. You can view the canyon from either the North Rim or the South Rim. Both sides are breathtaking. The South Rim attracts more visitors. The South Rim is easily accessible.

_____
_____
_____
_____
_____

2. You go outside at night. You can see the moon. Have you ever wondered why? The moon does not give off any light of its own. It appears very bright in the evening sky. We are able to see the moon. Sunlight reflects off its surface and into our eyes.

_____
_____
_____
_____

Name _____ Date _____

Homophones

Homophones are words that sound the same but have different spellings and meanings. Some examples of homophones include **son/sun**, **made/maid**, and **heard/herd**.

Talking is not **allowed** during the show.   **Allowed** means "permitted."
Therefore, nobody spoke **aloud**.   **Aloud** means "able to be heard."

**Circle the two words that sound the same in each sentence.
Then write the word that matches the definition.**

1. "How Bear Lost Its Tail" is my favorite tale.

   Story is another word for _____.

2. It is a principle of our school principal to know each student's name.

   A _____ is "a rule of conduct."

3. The completion of the work at the construction site is a welcome sight.

   Location is another word for _____.

4. Would you prefer a door made of wood or metal?

   Lumber is another word for _____.

5. I finished my algebra lesson on Friday to lessen my homework on Saturday.

   Reduce is another word for _____.

6. Whether we go snorkeling today or tomorrow depends on the weather.

   If is another word for _____.

7. In an incredible feat of strength, Calvin sprinted the last hundred feet.

   Achievement is another word for _____.

Homophones

Homophones are words that sound the same but have different spellings and meanings. Some examples of homophones include **to/two/too**, **there/their/they're**, and **passed/past**.

Whether or not we have the picnic depends on the **weather**.

Circle the two words that sound the same in each sentence. Then write the word that matches the definition.

1. I can't practice my new piece unless I have peace and quiet.

Calm is another word for _____.

2. There is no way we can play baseball in their small backyard.

_____ is a **pronoun**.

3. The parade always passed by our grandparents' house in past years.

Previous is another word for _____.

4. The bus fare from Cedar Road to the street fair is affordable.

Payment is another word for _____.

5. The scene from your window is the most lovely I've ever seen.

Viewed is another word for _____.

6. After he threw out the trash, Marlon was through with her chores.

Finished is another word for _____.

7. What's the best way to weigh a toddler who won't sit still?

Method is another word for _____.

8. The bus driver almost missed the exit to the farm because of the mist.

Overlooked is another word for _____.

Name _____ Date _____

Homophones

Homophones are words that sound the same but have different spellings and meanings. Some examples of homophones include contractions and possessive pronouns like the following: **they're/their**, **it's/its**, **you're/your**, **who's/whose**.

Contraction	**Possessive Pronoun**
they're = they are	their
it's = it is	its
you're = you are	your
who's = who is	whose

Write the contraction and the possessive pronoun of the words in the parentheses ( ) on the correct line to complete each sentence.

1. I know that _____ very busy, but I could use _____ help. (you are)

2. The students think _____ going to miss the start of school because

_____ bus is late.   (they are)

3. Do you know _____ playing in the football game tonight?   (who is)

4. _____ fun to watch my cat chasing _____ tail.   (it is)

5. Please raise _____ hand if _____ in the choir this year. (you are)

6. _____ markers are these? _____ missing their markers? (who is)

7. _____ going to tell me _____ bag this is? (who is)

8. I can't tell if _____ having a good time or if you would rather be at home

in _____ pajamas. (you are)

9. _____ back from _____ trip.   (they are)

Informal and Formal Language

Informal language consists of incomplete sentences and slang. Use informal language in friendly pieces of writing, such as an e-mail or a letter to a friend. Formal language consists of complete sentences and standard grammar. Use formal language in an essay or a letter to the editor.

Informal

Hey, wanna grab a bite to eat tonight?

Jay shouted, "Yo! It's been like a million years since I saw you last!"

Formal

I wish to extend an invitation for dinner this evening.

Jay said, "Hello, I have not seen you in a long time."

Circle whether each sentence is informal or formal.

1. Let's do something super fun after school!

informal   formal

2. I wish to inquire about the meeting that will be held later this week.

informal   formal

3. Rachel waved at me, and I said, "Later!"

informal   formal

4. The kid in the store was like, "Are you serious?"

informal   formal

5. I would appreciate your advice concerning this issue.

informal   formal

6. This movie is quite long, and I have an appointment in an hour.

informal   formal

Name _____ Date _____

Informal and Formal Language

Informal language consists of incomplete sentences and slang. Use informal language in friendly pieces of writing, such as an e-mail or a letter to a friend. Formal language consists of complete sentences and standard grammar. Use formal language in an essay or a letter to the editor.

Informal

A bunch of people went to the concert.

Formal

A group of people attended the concert.

Choose the formal word or phrase in the parentheses ( ).
Write it on the line.

1. The nobles _____ the needs of the common people.

(shrugged off, fully ignored)

2. The angry mob _____ as the nobles rode by.

(hollered, shouted)

3. The people _____ when the king ignored their petition.

(staged protests, acted up)

4. The king _____ why his subjects revolted.

(didn't get, did not understand)

5. The _____ needed new leadership.

(citizens, folks)

6. The minister _____ and then left the chamber.

(spoke convincingly, had his say)

Informal and Formal Language

Informal language consists of incomplete sentences and slang. Use informal language in friendly pieces of writing, such as an e-mail or a letter to a friend. Formal language consists of complete sentences and standard grammar. Use formal language in an essay or a letter to the editor.

Informal
Let's get out of here!

Formal
I think that we should leave now.

Choose the formal word or phrase in the parentheses ( ).
Write it on the line.

1. The leaders announced that the summit was _____.

(successful, a big hit)

2. The laws were _____ more outdated than anyone realized.

(a lot, considerably)

3. The city council chairperson tried to _____ everyone's opinion.

(do right by, respect)

4. If the new style of uniform _____, the school will officially adopt it.

(tests well, catches on)

5. As a sign of goodwill, the king _____ a holiday.

(said it's, declared)

6. Many people _____ the politician's point of view.

(disapproved of, couldn't stand)

7. The governor realized she should _____ the mayor at the meeting.

(acknowledge, say hi to)

Conquer Grammar • Grade 6 • © Newmark Learning, LLC

Informal and Formal Language

Informal language consists of incomplete sentences and slang. Use informal language in friendly pieces of writing, such as an e-mail or a letter to a friend. Formal language consists of complete sentences and standard grammar. Use formal language in an essay or a letter to the editor. Avoid using contractions such as **I'm** or **won't** in formal pieces of writing.

Informal
Hey, I'm sorry, but Mr. Florian won't be able to make it.

Formal
I regret to inform you that Mr. Florian will not be able to attend.

Rewrite each sentence. Replace the underlined words with formal language.

1. <u>Huh</u>, how come the concert <u>got</u> canceled?

   _____

2. I <u>totally love</u> flying <u>wherever.</u>

   _____

3. Cancun, Mexico, is a <u>sweet</u> place to visit.

   _____

4. An active volcano is the <u>coolest thing</u>.

   _____

5. If traveling by plane <u>isn't your thing</u>, there's <u>tons</u> to see closer to home.

   _____

   _____

6. Seeing spiders in person <u>freaks me out</u>.

   _____

Informal and Formal Language

Informal language consists of incomplete sentences and slang. Use informal language in friendly pieces of writing, such as an e-mail or a letter to a friend. Formal language consists of complete sentences and standard grammar. Use formal language in an essay or a letter to the editor. Avoid using contractions such as **I'm** or **won't** in formal pieces of writing.

Informal	**Formal**
You've really got to move a lot to stay in shape.	People need to exercise often to stay healthy.

Rewrite each sentence. Replace the informal language with formal language.

1. Think you don't need exercise? You're totally wrong.

_____

2. Exercise is super good for your heart.

_____

3. A good workout leaves you feeling a lot more mellow.

_____

4. Working out is a really awesome way to get fit.

_____

5. If using machines isn't your thing, chill out and find another way to work out.

_____

_____

6. You can read loads of books as you cycle on the stationary bike.

_____

Name _____ Date _____

Informal and Formal Language

Informal language consists of incomplete sentences and slang. Use informal language in friendly pieces of writing, such as an e-mail or a letter to a friend. Formal language consists of complete sentences and standard grammar. Use formal language in an essay or a letter to the editor. Avoid using contractions such as **I'm** or **won't** in formal pieces of writing.

Informal
The sixth-grade kids brought in lots of muffins for the bake sale.

Formal
The sixth-grade students brought in many muffins for the bake sale.

Rewrite each sentence. Replace the informal language with formal language.

1. Wow, the cop who spoke at our school today was awesome.

_____

2. All the kids thought the stuff she said was cool.

_____

3. Did you learn a heap from her talk?

_____

4. Sophie's dad works at the fire station a couple of blocks away.

_____

5. If we send him an invite to our class, I'm guessing he'd show up.

_____

6. Man, I want to know literally all the info about being a firefighter.

_____

Standard English

Standard English is the language used in academic writing and in classrooms. It follows accepted rules of grammar, punctuation, spelling, and vocabulary. Nonstandard or conversational English is used in informal communication, such as text messages, e-mails, and story dialogue.

Each sentence has one error in spelling, punctuation, or grammar. Rewrite each sentence, applying the rules of standard English.

1. Felicia wrote a letter to the editor she wants everyone to vote for her mom.

_____

2. Both Winnie and Yuki did well on her assignments.

_____

3. The archaeologists found rare artifacts at the new sight.

_____

4. Gianni said that he once faced a similar problem hisself.

_____

5. By the time the downpour began, I were at home.

_____

6. The movie about the boy who wanted to be a firefighter.

_____

7. Do you know who's snacks are on the table?

_____

Standard English

Standard English is the language used in academic writing and in classrooms.
It follows accepted rules of grammar, punctuation, spelling, and vocabulary.
Nonstandard or conversational English is used in informal communication,
such as text messages, e-mails, and story dialogue.

Rewrite each sentence, applying the rules of standard English.

1. If it ain't broke, don't fix it.

_____

2. Raj finished his homework real fast because he wanted to

hang out with his friends.

_____

_____

3. I need to find the article about them heroes.

_____

4. The students want that there rule about cell phones to be changed.

_____

5. I think that sometimes nature be better than civilization.

_____

6. My dad he claim that the 1980s were the golden age of popular music.

_____

Standard English

Standard English is the language used in academic writing and in classrooms. It follows accepted rules of grammar, punctuation, spelling, and vocabulary. Nonstandard or conversational English is used in informal communication, such as text messages, e-mails, and story dialogue.

Rewrite the letter using standard English grammar, spelling, punctuation, and vocabulary. Errors in standard English are underlined.

Dear Editor,

   Students for Bridge Park would like to invite the entire city to come out on Sunday to support <u>are</u> local park. Bridge Park is <u>a way big</u> contributor to city life. Each year, thousands of people <u>visits</u> the park to swim, hike, or ride <u>there</u> bicycles. The <u>parks</u> many acres also support local species from historic old trees to colorful flocks of birds to a large <u>heard</u> of <u>deers</u>.

   On Sunday, our class <u>are</u> holding a picnic to raise money for Bridge Park. The money will go toward additional <u>childrens</u> activities. We hope to <u>insure</u> that the park will always be a <u>cool</u> place for people of all ages.

Sincerely,

The Sixth Grade Class

_____

_____

_____

_____

_____

_____

_____

_____

_____

_____

Standard English

Standard English is the language used in academic writing and in classrooms. It follows accepted rules of grammar, punctuation, spelling, and vocabulary. Nonstandard or conversational English is used in informal communication, such as text messages, e-mails, and story dialogue.

Rewrite the passage, applying the rules of standard English.

The rice paddies of china the philippines and japan is considered engineering feets of the ancient world. People have growed rice for thousands of years. About 2,000, years ago rice growers in asia began building terraced paddies. The terraces allowed the farmers to grow his rice on the sides of hills and mountains. These here terraced steps saved both space and water.

To water the rice, the farmers built a complex system of canals. The irrigation system still be used today. Water flows down the terraces, irrigating each field as it go. The young rice plants sits in fields with about six inch of water? As the rice matures, the guys can drop the water level. When the rice is ready, the ground is dry. Then the rice can be harvested nice and easy.

_____

_____

_____

_____

_____

_____

_____

_____

Answer Key

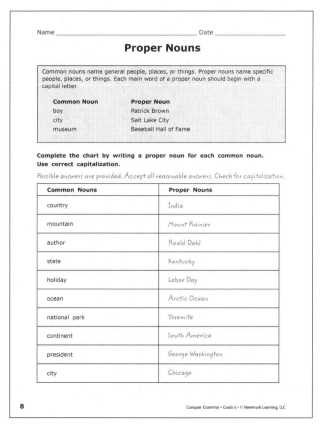

Page 8

Proper Nouns

Common nouns name general people, places, or things. Proper nouns name specific people, places, or things. Each main word of a proper noun should begin with a capital letter.

Common Noun	Proper Noun
boy	Patrick Brown
city	Salt Lake City
museum	Baseball Hall of Fame

Complete the chart by writing a proper noun for each common noun. Use correct capitalization.

Possible answers are provided. Accept all reasonable answers. Check for capitalization.

Common Nouns	Proper Nouns
country	India
mountain	Mount Rainier
author	Roald Dahl
state	Kentucky
holiday	Labor Day
ocean	Arctic Ocean
national park	Yosemite
continent	South America
president	George Washington
city	Chicago

8   Conquer Grammar • Grade 6 • © Newmark Learning, LLC

Page 9

Plural Nouns

A plural noun names more than one person, place, or thing. Add **s** to the end of most nouns to make them plural. For nouns ending in **x, z, s, sh,** or **ch,** add **-es.** For nouns ending in a consonant and **y,** change the **y** to **i** and add **-es.** For nouns ending in **f** or **fe,** change the last letter to **v** and then add **-es.**

Singular Noun	Plural Noun
cat	cats
lady	ladies
fly	flies
loaf	loaves
life	lives

Write the plural form of the noun in the parentheses ( ) to complete each sentence.

1. Don't you agree that Aunt Gloria throws the best __parties__? (party)

2. My little brothers jumped into the piles of __leaves__ in the yard. (leaf)

3. Grandmother polished her antique silver spoons, forks, and __knives__. (knife)

4. We saw the newest __calves__ in the pasture. (calf)

5. Benjamin showed me his huge collection of __pennies__. (penny)

6. The wild horses' __hooves__ made a thundering noise as the herd ran by. (hoof)

7. The __shelves__ were packed with books. (shelf)

8. The __puppies__ jumped onto the chair. (puppy)

Conquer Grammar • Grade 6 • © Newmark Learning, LLC   9

Page 10

Irregular Plural Nouns

The plural form of some nouns is irregular because there are no clear spelling rules to follow when forming the plural. Sometimes a noun's spelling doesn't change at all.

Singular Noun	Plural Noun
man	men
foot	feet
offspring	offspring
salmon	salmon
louse	lice

Circle the plural noun in the parentheses ( ) that correctly completes each sentence. If necessary, use a dictionary for help.

1. We caught many (**trout**, trouts) on our last fishing trip.

2. My friend in Canada often sees a flock of (goose, **geese**) in her yard.

3. Once in awhile, she may see several (**moose**, meese) from her window.

4. The Saturday matinee was filled with hundreds of (**children**, childs).

5. Do you think we will see some (**deer**, deers) grazing in the meadow?

6. The (workmans, **workmen**) helped build the tallest building in town.

7. Despite being very excited, the (**people**, persons) in the crowd didn't make much noise.

8. The (woman, **women**) worked together to repair the broken fence.

10   Conquer Grammar • Grade 6 • © Newmark Learning, LLC

Page 11

Possessive Nouns

A possessive noun tells who or what owns something.
Use **'s** to show possession for one person, place, or thing.
    The toy belongs to the cat. It is the **cat's** toy.

Use **s'** to show possession for more than one person, place, or thing.
    The cat belongs to my two sisters. It is my **sisters'** cat.

Use **'s** to show possession to a noun with an irregular plural form.
    The **schoolchildren's** teacher was absent today.

Circle the possessive noun in each sentence. Then write whether it is singular or plural.

1. My (**grandfather's**) truck was filled with camping supplies. __singular__

2. The (**geese's**) honking could be heard from a mile away. __plural__

3. All of the (**tourists'**) photos were of the same landmark. __plural__

4. Unfortunately, the (**women's**) team practice was canceled today. __plural__

5. I couldn't believe how long that (**giraffe's**) neck really was! __singular__

6. The (**trees'**) fruit was ready to be harvested. __plural__

Conquer Grammar • Grade 6 • © Newmark Learning, LLC   11

Answer Key

Name _____ Date _____

Present Perfect Tense

The present perfect tense tells about an action that starts in the past and continues into the present. It can also tell about changes or experiences that happen over a period of time. The present perfect tense uses the helping verbs **has** or **have** with the past tense of a main verb.
Lindsay **has loved** to sing as long as we all can remember.
Winston and Walter **have played** on the soccer team since last year.

Rewrite each sentence with the present perfect tense of the verb in the parentheses ( ).

1. I (wash) my own laundry since I was nine years old.

   I have washed my own laundry since I was nine years old.

2. Mom thinks you (outgrow) your bicycle, and she said I can have it.

   Mom thinks you have outgrown your bicycle, and she said I can have it.

3. Richard (complete) his hike along the Appalachian Trail.

   Richard has completed his hike along the Appalachian Trail.

4. Daryll and Diana (learn) to snowboard in time for their vacation.

   Daryll and Diana have learned to snowboard in time for their vacation.

5. With this trip, Jason's dad (visit) every national park in California.

   With this trip, Jason's dad has visited every national park in California.

6. Because she will visit France, Rory (decide) to learn French.

   Because she will visit France, Rory has decided to learn French.

7. The construction team (work) hard to complete the bridge within budget.

   The construction team has worked hard to complete the bridge within budget.

8. The twins (open) all of their presents and now we will eat cake and ice cream.

   The twins have opened all of their presents and now we will eat cake and ice cream.

Conquer Grammar • Grade 6 • © Newmark Learning, LLC

Page 12

Name _____ Date _____

Perfect Tenses

The present perfect tense tells about an action that starts in the past and continues into the present. It can also tell about changes or experiences that happen over a period of time. The present perfect tense uses the helping verbs **has** or **have** with the past tense of a main verb.
Present perfect: William **has played** the drums and clarinet since September.

The past perfect tense tells about an action that starts and ends in the past. The past perfect tense uses the helping verb **had** with the past tense of a main verb.
Past perfect: By the end of summer, he **had learned** to play the violin.

The future perfect tense tells about an action that starts in the past and continues into the future. The future perfect tense uses the helping verbs **will have** with the past tense of a main verb.
Future perfect: By next year, he **will have mastered** three instruments.

Rewrite each sentence with the indicated tense of the underlined verb.

1. My mom <u>serve</u> perfect meatballs since I can remember. (present perfect)

   My mom has served perfect meatballs since I can remember.

2. Nana <u>teach</u> her to make them by the time Mom was my age. (past perfect)

   Nana had taught her to make them by the time Mom was my age.

3. My grandmother <u>live</u> with us for the past three months. (present perfect)

   My grandmother has lived with us for the past three months.

4. After next week, Mom and Dad <u>renew</u> their wedding vows. (future perfect)

   After next week, Mom and Dad will have renewed their wedding vows.

5. I hope in twenty years, I <u>find</u> a true love like theirs. (future perfect)

   I hope in twenty years, I will have found a true love like theirs.

6. Nana <u>discover</u> the recipe written on her mother's tattered index card. (past perfect)

   Nana had discovered the recipe written on her mother's tattered index card.

Conquer Grammar • Grade 6 • © Newmark Learning, LLC

Page 13

Name _____ Date _____

Literary Present Tense

When describing the events that occur in a story or a play, use the present tense or the literary present.

In *Annie*, the main character **is** a young girl who **lives** in an orphanage.

For each passage, underline the form of the verb in the parentheses ( ) that is in the literary present.

1. In *Romeo and Juliet*, one of Shakespeare's most famous plays, the two main characters meet at a party and (fell, <u>fall</u>) in love. The problem is that their families (<u>hate</u>, hated) each other. Romeo and Juliet (<u>know</u>, knew) they will not be allowed to marry. However, Friar Laurence kindly (helped, <u>helps</u>) them marry in secret. Then something terrible (happened, <u>happens</u>). The day after the wedding, Romeo (<u>kills</u>, killed) Juliet's cousin in a duel. In the morning he (<u>is</u>, was) forced to leave Juliet. Romeo (<u>cannot</u>, could not) return to the city, or else he will be put to death.

2. In *Because of Winn-Dixie* by Kate DiCamillo, ten-year-old Opal Buloni (<u>has</u>, had) just moved to a new town in Florida. She (was, <u>is</u>) lonely and missing her mother who left when Opal was only three years old. Opal (<u>is wondering</u>, was wondering) how she is going to make it through the long, hot summer when she (<u>finds</u>, found) a big dog in a Winn-Dixie grocery store. She (named, <u>names</u>) the dog Winn-Dixie and (<u>takes</u>, took) him home to meet her father.

Conquer Grammar • Grade 6 • © Newmark Learning, LLC

Page 14

Name _____ Date _____

Literary Present Tense

When describing the events that occur in a story or a play, use the present tense or the literary present.

In *The Giver*, Jonas **is** a boy who **stores** his community's memories.

Complete the essay. Write the literary present tense form of the verb in the parentheses ( ).

In the novel *Tuck Everlasting*, by Natalie Babbitt, the members of the Tuck family have eternal life because they _drink_ water from a
(to drink)
magic spring. The family _moves_ from place to place. They _live_
(to move)   (lived)
so quietly that their neighbors don't realize that there is something odd about the family.

Then ten-year-old Winnie Foster accidentally _discovers_ the Tucks'
(to discover)
secret. The Tucks _try_ to explain why remaining the same age
(to try)
forever isn't as wonderful as it _seems_. The plot thickens when a
(to seem)
stranger _arrives_. He has a plan. He _wants_ to market the spring
(to arrive)   (wanted)
water.

Conquer Grammar • Grade 6 • © Newmark Learning, LLC

Page 15

Answer Key

Name _____ Date _____

Verp Tenses / Verb Tenses

Page 16

Name _____ Date _____

Verb Tenses

Present tense verbs tell about something that is happening right now. Past tense verbs tell about something that has already happened. Future tense verbs tell about something that will happen at a later time.

Present: I **exercise** after school.
Past: Yesterday, I **exercised** with my friend.
Future: I **will exercise** every day next week.

For each sentence, determine when the action is happening. Choose the verb in parentheses ( ) that correctly completes the sentence and write it on the line.

1. I am going to the community center, and I _____will study_____ with my friends.
(will study, studied)

2. Tomorrow, we _____will go_____ out for dinner, and then we will visit Mara.
(will go, went)

3. I _____ate_____ a sandwich even though I had already eaten lunch.
(eat, ate)

4. When Mr. Sansone arrives, he _____will give_____ out the awards.
(will give, gives)

5. The Nile River, which is in Africa, _____rises_____ south of the Equator and flows north.
(rises, rose)

6. The two rivals _____met_____ to resolve their differences.
(are meeting, met)

7. In the novel, the main character is stunned when she first _____sees_____ her long-lost friend.
(sees, saw)

16   Conquer Grammar • Grade 6 • © Newmark Learning, LLC

Page 17

Name _____ Date _____

Shifts in Verb Tense

Present tense verbs tell about something that is happening right now. Past tense verbs tell about something that has already happened. Future tense verbs tell about something that will happen at a later time. Change tenses to describe actions that happen at different times.

The children **hiked** all day and **are** now resting by the campfire.

Underline the verbs that shift tenses in each sentence.

1. The sun <u>rose</u> early, but the air <u>is</u> still cool.

2. I <u>will stay</u> in my sleeping bag until I <u>hear</u> the other campers talking.

3. We <u>heard</u> strange sounds last night and now everyone <u>thinks</u> there are bears around.

4. I <u>slept</u> well last night, however, I <u>will sleep</u> poorly tonight!

5. Mila <u>ran</u> a race, and now she <u>is</u> resting.

Write the correct form of the verb in the parentheses ( ) to complete each sentence.

6. Today was rainy, but we hope tomorrow _____will be_____ sunny.
(to be)

7. We started the campfire in the morning and it still _____burns_____ brightly.
(burn)

8. I brought my dog, Rex, on the trip because my friends _____like_____ him a lot.
(like)

9. We love being in the wilderness, but we _____will return_____ home later today.
(return)

Conquer Grammar • Grade 6 • © Newmark Learning, LLC   17

Page 18

Name _____ Date _____

Shifts in Verb Tense

Present tense verbs tell about something that is happening right now. Past tense verbs tell about something that has already happened. Future tense verbs tell about something that will happen at a later time. Change tenses to describe actions that happen at different times.

We **are** surprised that the movie **had** a happy ending.
The staff **will pop** more popcorn because they just **sold** the last bag.

Circle the correct verb to complete each sentence.

1. I called my friend to ask if she (went, (will go)) with me to see the movie.

2. I will want company if the movie (was, (is)) scary!

3. We arrived late, but the trailers ((are,) will be) still running.

4. I usually walk to school, but yesterday I (ride, (rode)) my bike.

5. After I eat dinner, I ((will play,) played) the piano.

6. We played basketball this morning, but now we ((are,) were) resting.

7. I already ate my lunch, so I (buy, (will buy)) a snack.

8. As soon as I get to the beach, I ((will jump,) jump) in the ocean.

9. We will play checkers while we ((wait,) will wait) for the storm to pass.

18   Conquer Grammar • Grade 6 • © Newmark Learning, LLC

Page 19

Name _____ Date _____

Shifts in Verb Tense

Present tense verbs tell about something that is happening right now. Past tense verbs tell about something that has already happened. Future tense verbs tell about something that will happen at a later time. Change tenses to describe actions that happen at different times.

The sky **is** clear now, but maybe it **will rain** later.

Choose the correct verb in the parentheses ( ). Write it on the line.

1. After we eat lunch, we (walked, will walk) the dogs. _____will walk_____

2. The dogs played, and now they (are, were) snoozing. _____are_____

3. I finished my book report, and now I (played, play) my guitar. _____play_____

4. We planted bulbs that (bloomed, will bloom) in March. _____will bloom_____

Rewrite the passage. Use the literary present tense of the verbs in the parentheses ( ).

Encyclopedia Brown books (to feature) a boy detective, Leroy Brown. His nickname is "Encyclopedia," because he (to be) very intelligent and well-read. Most of the books in the series (to begin) with Leroy having dinner with his father, the police chief of a small town. The chief (to describe) his current case to his son. Leroy (to ask) a question or two. Then he (to solve) the mystery right at the dinner table.

Encyclopedia Brown books feature a boy detective, Leroy Brown. His nickname is "Encyclopedia," because he is very intelligent and well-read. Most of the books in the series begin with Leroy having dinner with his father, the police chief of a small town. The chief describes his current case to his son. Leroy asks a question or two. Then he solves the mystery right at the dinner table.

Conquer Grammar • Grade 6 • © Newmark Learning, LLC   19

Answer Key

Page 20

Name _____ Date _____

Subject-Verb Agreement

The subject of a sentence is a noun that tells who or what the sentence is about. The verb tells what the subject does. The subject and the verb of a sentence must agree. A singular subject takes a singular verb. A plural subject, including a compound subject, takes a plural verb.

Singular Subject: A student from our class **is** in the talent show.
Plural Subject: Ms. Jeffries and Mr. Thomas often **attend** the meetings.
Compound Subject: The committee members **hope** lots of students will participate.

Underline the subject of each sentence. Then choose the verb in the parentheses ( ) that agrees with the subject and write it on the line.

1. The list of story-starters __is__ on the board.
   (is, are)

2. Dean and Maisha __are__ co-chairs of the advisory board.
   (is, are)

3. The members of the board __have agreed__ to meet again next week.
   (has agreed, have agreed)

4. Mark and I __were__ excited to meet our favorite ice hockey player.
   (was, were)

5. One of the shirts __is__ a large, and two are mediums.
   (is, are)

6. I __am going__ to the observatory tomorrow night.
   (am going, is going)

7. We __understand__ why you are frustrated about the results.
   (understands, understand)

8. Rita and Drew __intend__ to write a letter to the editor about the issue.
   (intends, intend)

20   Conquer Grammar • Grade 6 • © Newmark Learning, LLC

Page 21

Name _____ Date _____

Subject-Verb Agreement

The subject of a sentence is a noun that tells who or what the sentence is about. The verb tells what the subject does. The subject and the verb of a sentence must agree. A singular subject takes a singular verb. A plural subject, including a compound subject, takes a plural verb.

Singular Subject: The list of suggested books **is** online.
Plural Subject: Hardbacks and paperbacks of all genres **are** available in our library.
Compound Subject: Louise and May **take** out books often.

Underline the subject of each sentence. Then choose the verb in the parentheses ( ) that agrees with the subject and write it on the line.

1. Mary and Celine __are__ the strongest players on our team.
   (is, are)

2. The teammates __have voted__ in favor of Saturday practice.
   (has voted, have voted)

3. The schedule of after-school clubs __was announced__ yesterday.
   (was announced, were announced)

4. Before a Spanish test, Melissa and I usually __quiz__ each other on vocabulary.
   (quizzes, quiz)

5. Two of the students __are going__ to sing a solo.
   (is going, are going)

6. The administrators __meet__ every Thursday afternoon.
   (meets, meet)

7. The lesson topics for the next two weeks __have been posted__ online.
   (has been posted, have been posted)

21   Conquer Grammar • Grade 6 • © Newmark Learning, LLC

Page 22

Name _____ Date _____

Subject-Verb Agreement

The subject of a sentence is a noun that tells who or what the sentence is about. The verb tells what the subject does. The subject and the verb of a sentence must agree. A singular subject takes a singular verb. A plural subject, including a compound subject, takes a plural verb.

Singular Subject: Marty **goes** to the store.
Plural Subject: We **are** thrilled to be invited to the championship game.
Compound Subject: You and I **have** lunch at noon.

Complete each sentence. Circle the verb in the parentheses ( ) that agrees with the subject of the sentence and write it on the line.

1. All players __are__ to be on the field at 11 a.m. (is, (are))

2. Nyla, who is my neighbor, and I __have__ known each other since we were in the first grade. (has, (have))

3. An elephant __is__ a very intelligent animal. ((is) are)

4. Mabel, who's on the school paper, and I __have__ interviewed the custodian. (has, (have))

5. I __want__ to visit my grandfather on Tuesday. ((want) wants)

6. Maura, Kelly, and Rahim __are__ running for class president. (is, (are))

7. We __do__ understand your perspective, but we disagree. (does, (do))

8. Shayla and I __were__ excited to meet our favorite author. (was, (were))

22   Conquer Grammar • Grade 6 • © Newmark Learning, LLC

Page 23

Name _____ Date _____

Subject-Verb Agreement

The subject of a sentence is a noun that tells who or what the sentence is about. The verb tells what the subject does. The subject and the verb of a sentence must agree. A singular subject takes a singular verb. A plural subject, including a compound subject, takes a plural verb.

Singular Subject: Molly **takes** the city bus home.
Plural Subject: Edgar and Bob **take** it, too.
Compound Subject: They **will walk** next week.

Circle the verb in the parentheses ( ) that agrees with the subject of the sentence. Then write it on the line.

1. They __are__ ready when you are. (is, (are))

2. You __have__ the stopwatch. (has, (have))

3. Lisette and I __are__ volunteering at the animal shelter. (am, (are))

4. A puppy rarely __sits__ still for more than five minutes. (sit, (sits))

5. You still __do__ not realize the depth of the problem. (does, (do))

6. Alia __is__ bringing beverages to the picnic. (am, (is))

7. Rocco and Mia __were__ almost home when it began to rain. (was, (were))

8. It __takes__ time to write a clever story. (take, (takes))

9. A tutor __helps__ a student with homework. (help, (helps))

10. I like to __go__ out for lunch. ((go) goes)

23   Conquer Grammar • Grade 6 • © Newmark Learning, LLC

Answer Key

Name _____ Date _____

Subject-Verb Agreement

The subject of a sentence is a noun that tells who or what the sentence is about. The verb tells what the subject does. The subject and the verb of a sentence must agree. A singular subject takes a singular verb. A plural subject, including a compound subject, takes a plural verb.

Singular Subject: Alejandro **rehearses** for the play every Monday and Thursday.
Plural Subject: Kyle and Misha **are** in charge of costumes.
Compound Subject: Nicky, who is my best friend, and I **are** in the band.

Complete each sentence. Choose the verb in the parentheses ( ) that agrees with the subject of the sentence and write it on the line.

1. The clarinet players in the band ___practice___ together on Saturday.
   (practices, practice)

2. The president ___says___ that he will address the nation.
   (says, say)

3. The director of the event ___deserves___ a round of applause.
   (deserves, deserve)

4. Three of the fish ___are___ striped and one is solid orange.
   (is, are)

5. The fans who watched the game ___agree___ that it was very disappointing.
   (agrees, agree)

6. All the neighbors who donated ___have brought___ warm clothing.
   (has brought, have brought)

7. Everybody ___contributes___ in a different way.
   (contribute, contributes)

24

Conquer Grammar • Grade 6 • © Newmark Learning, LLC

Page 24

Name _____ Date _____

Subject-Verb Agreement

The subject of a sentence is a noun that tells who or what the sentence is about. The verb tells what the subject does. The subject and the verb of a sentence must agree. A singular subject takes a singular verb. A plural subject, including a compound subject, takes a plural verb.

Singular Subject: The list of reference books **is** in your folder.
Plural Subject: Victor and Luis **want** to go to the playoff game.
Compound Subject: Physicians **agree** that learning new things is good for your brain.

Rewrite each sentence with correct subject-verb agreement.

1. The historians speaks at the museum today.
   The historians speak at the museum today.

2. The field hockey players practices in the upper field.
   The field hockey players practice in the upper field.

3. The citizens of Springfield has a new mayor.
   The citizens of Springfield have a new mayor.

4. Margie and Kevin is at the train station.
   Margie and Kevin are at the train station.

5. The best bands in the city marches in the parade.
   The best bands in the city march in the parade.

6. The chickens was running through the yard.
   The chickens were running through the yard.

7. My sister decide what to watch.
   My sister decides what to watch.

Conquer Grammar • Grade 6 • © Newmark Learning, LLC

25

Page 25

Name _____ Date _____

Subject Pronouns

A pronoun is a word that takes the place of a noun. **I, you, she, he, it, we,** and **they** are subject pronouns. Use a subject pronoun when a pronoun is the subject of a sentence.

Incorrect: Her is my friend.
Correct: She is my friend.

Incorrect: My brother and **me** walk the dog twice a day.
Correct: My brother and **I** walk the dog twice a day.

Circle the correct subject pronoun in the parentheses ( ) to complete each sentence.

1. (Her, (She)) and Isabella are out riding skateboards.

2. Klaus and ((I), me) will go to the library with you on Thursday.

3. (Him, (He)) and (me, (I)) are building a doghouse.

4. ((They), Them) and the other tourists boarded the bus at dawn.

Circle the incorrect pronoun in each sentence.
Then rewrite the sentence with the correct subject pronoun.

5. (Us) and the mayor attended the grand opening.
   We and the mayor attended the grand opening.

6. Gil and (me) decided to work on the puzzle together.
   Gil and I decided to work on the puzzle together.

7. Suki and (her) made a cake.
   Suki and she made a cake.

8. My sister and (me) play board games.
   My sister and I play board games.

26

Conquer Grammar • Grade 6 • © Newmark Learning, LLC

Page 26

Name _____ Date _____

Object Pronouns

A pronoun is a word that takes the place of a noun. **Me, you, him, her, it, us,** and **them** are object pronouns. Use an object pronoun when a pronoun is the object of a verb or a preposition.

Incorrect: The art teacher encouraged Samantha and **I**.
Correct: The art teacher encouraged Samantha and **me**.

Incorrect: This is an important moment for us and **they**.
Correct: This is an important moment for us and **them**.

Circle the correct object pronoun in the parentheses ( ) to complete each sentence.

1. Marina is writing a story about (he, (him)) and his brother.

2. Jamie rides the subway with my friend and (I, (me)).

3. Finn sent letters to you and (we, (us)).

4. That shouldn't be a matter of (we, (us)) against ((them) they).

Circle the incorrect pronoun or pronouns in each sentence.
Then rewrite the sentence with the correct object pronoun.

5. Angel went to the play with Cory and (I).
   Angel went to the play with Cory and me.

6. Mr. Lu coached (he) and her.
   Mr. Lu coached him and her.

7. Ava gave Nora and (I) some fruit.
   Ava gave Nora and me some fruit.

8. Remember to text (she) and (I).
   Remember to text her and me.

Conquer Grammar • Grade 6 • © Newmark Learning, LLC

27

Page 27

96

Answer Key

Page 28

Name _____ Date _____

Possessive Pronouns

Pronouns take the place of nouns. A possessive pronoun shows who or what owns something. **My, mine, your, yours, her, hers, his, its, our, ours, their,** and **theirs** are possessive pronouns. A possessive pronoun should never have an apostrophe.

This is not **my** backpack. That red one is **mine**.
This dog is **theirs**. I'm taking it back to **their** house.

Circle the possessive pronoun or pronouns in the parentheses ( ) that correctly complete each sentence.

1. The dog chased (its, their) toy.

2. Andy unlocked the door of (his, hers) house.

3. Craig, is this binder (yours, your)?

4. I would like (my, mine) notes back in an hour, please.

5. The two friends decided to eat (their, theirs) lunches together.

6. I finished (mine, my) ice cream. Are you done with (your, yours)?

7. We can have the reunion at (your, yours) house or (our, ours).

8. That dark green backpack is (my, mine), but the green one is (her, hers).

9. The students claimed the library study room as (theirs, their) from 1 p.m. to 3 p.m.

10. I see that (my, mine) plant needs more water, for (its, their) leaves are turning brown.

Conquer Grammar • Grade 6 • © Newmark Learning, LLC

Page 28

Page 29

Name _____ Date _____

Possessive Pronouns

Pronouns take the place of nouns. A possessive pronoun shows who or what owns something. **My, mine, your, yours, her, hers, his, its, our, ours, their,** and **theirs** are possessive pronouns. A possessive pronoun should never have an apostrophe.

We have **our** tickets. These three are **ours**.
Her seat is in row B. The seat on the aisle is **hers**.

Circle the correct possessive pronoun. Then write it on the line.

1. Luisa spoke of _____her_____ adventures in the Arctic. (her, hers)

2. Mrs. O'Malley said I could have an extra day to write _____my_____ paper. (my, mine)

3. Jamal turned to me and asked, "Is this notebook mine or _____yours_____?" (your, yours)

4. My family moved into _____our_____ new house last month. (our, ours)

5. The cats treated the orphaned kitten as if it were _____theirs_____. (their, theirs)

For each pair of sentences, circle the possessive pronoun in the first sentence and complete the second sentence with the correct form of the same pronoun.

6. These are (our) ideas. These ideas are _____ours_____.

7. Is this apple (yours)? Is this _____your_____ apple?

8. That scarf looks just like (my) scarf. That scarf looks just like _____mine_____.

Conquer Grammar • Grade 6 • © Newmark Learning, LLC   29

Page 29

Page 30

Name _____ Date _____

Possessive Pronouns

Pronouns take the place of nouns. A possessive pronoun shows who or what owns something. **My, mine, your, yours, her, hers, his, its, our, ours, their,** and **theirs** are possessive pronouns. A possessive pronoun should never have an apostrophe. A contraction always has an apostrophe. Possessive pronouns and contractions are frequently confused.

Possessive Pronoun	Contraction
its	it's (it is)
your	you're (you are)
their	they're (they are)
whose	who's (who is)

Complete each sentence. Write the contraction and the possessive pronoun in the parentheses ( ) on the correct line.

1. If you miss _____your_____ connection, _____you're_____ going to be late. (you're, your)

2. Did you say _____they're_____ riding _____their_____ surfboards in a competition? (they're, their)

3. _____Whose_____ e-mail asked, "_____who's_____ your favorite actor?" (Who's, Whose)

4. Stephen and Darin said _____they're_____ calling _____their_____ dad to come pick them up. (their, they're)

5. _____Whose_____ suitcase is this? _____Who's_____ going to use the treadmill? (Who's, Whose)

6. Ms. Chen said that _____you're_____ going to lend her _____your_____ book. (you're, your)

7. I think _____it's_____ unlucky that I dropped the phone and broke _____its_____ screen. (its, it's)

Conquer Grammar • Grade 6 • © Newmark Learning, LLC

Page 30

Page 31

Name _____ Date _____

Intensive Pronouns

An intensive pronoun emphasizes a noun or another pronoun in a sentence, but can be dropped without changing the meaning of the sentence. Intensive pronouns always end in either **-self** or **-selves**. **Myself, yourself, himself, herself, itself, ourselves, yourselves,** and **themselves** are intensive pronouns.

He knows where the box is because he **himself** moved it.
After watching the movie, I wanted to read the book **itself**.

Circle the intensive pronoun in each sentence. Then underline the noun or pronoun to which the intensive pronoun refers.

1. I (myself) opened the jar.

2. You (yourself) agreed to bring donations for the food pantry.

3. The farmer (himself) cleaned the chicken coop.

4. We heard the updated information from the principal (herself).

Write the correct intensive pronoun to complete each sentence. Choose one of the following: themselves, herself, itself, yourself.

5. Roxy _____herself_____ created the masterpiece.

6. The hamster _____itself_____ knocked over its food dish.

7. The volunteers _____themselves_____ weeded the entire community garden.

8. You _____yourself_____ said that you wanted to go to a concert.

Conquer Grammar • Grade 6 • © Newmark Learning, LLC   31

Page 31

Answer Key

Page 32

Name _____ Date _____

Intensive Pronouns

An intensive pronoun emphasizes a noun or another pronoun in a sentence, but can be dropped without changing the meaning of the sentence. Intensive pronouns always end in either **-self** or **-selves**. **Myself, yourself, himself, herself, itself, ourselves, yourselves,** and **themselves** are intensive pronouns.

Donna sent the mayor **himself** an invitation to the school play.
I **myself** stood in line to buy the tickets.

Write the correct intensive pronoun to complete each sentence. Choose one of the following: Myself, yourself, himself, herself, itself, ourselves, yourselves, themselves.

1. The choir members _themselves_ haven't heard the good news yet.

2. We _ourselves_ liked the book even though it didn't get a good review.

3. The crowd cheered as the Olympian _himself_ waved to them.

4. You _yourself_ agreed to mow the lawn.

5. My aunt _herself_ built the bunk beds.

6. Mr. Gupta invited the students _themselves_ to teach tomorrow's lesson.

7. I _myself_ was surprised when my apple pie won first place.

8. Although the setting was quite plain, I loved the story _itself_.

9. The playground _itself_ was newly constructed.

10. Mia invited Luke _himself_ to the movie.

32 | Conquer Grammar • Grade 6 • © Newmark Learning, LLC

Page 33

Name _____ Date _____

Intensive Pronouns

An intensive pronoun emphasizes a noun or another pronoun in a sentence, but can be dropped without changing the meaning of the sentence. Intensive pronouns always end in either **-self** or **-selves**. **Myself, yourself, himself, herself, itself, ourselves, yourselves,** and **themselves** are intensive pronouns.

You **yourselves** can make the posters for the book sale.
We **ourselves** can unpack all the books.

Write the correct intensive pronoun to complete each sentence. Choose one of the following: Myself, yourself, himself, herself, itself, ourselves, yourselves, themselves.

1. You _yourself_ should ask the advisor about joining the debate team.

2. The friends _themselves_ chose their new theme song.

3. We interviewed the lead actor _himself_ about his new play.

4. The chef _herself_ spoke to our club about her new cookbook.

5. I _myself_ would like to be a pilot someday.

6. We _ourselves_ made a project for the science fair.

7. The news channel ran a story about the school fair _itself_.

8. Brendan _himself_ painted his room a new color.

9. Mrs. Brant _herself_ should organize a class trip to the museum.

10. I _myself_ enjoyed looking at the photographs in the gallery.

11. The campers _themselves_ marched through the woods to the lake.

12. Mary _herself_ went to pick up the supplies at the hardware store.

Conquer Grammar • Grade 6 • © Newmark Learning, LLC | 33

Page 34

Name _____ Date _____

Pronoun-Antecedent Agreement

The noun that a pronoun replaces is called an antecedent. A pronoun and its antecedent must agree in number and person.

	Pronoun	Antecedent	Agreement
I put the book in **my** bag.	my	I	singular, first person
Sari, here are **your** test results.	your	Sari	singular, second person
The **students** wanted to help, so **they** organized a lake clean-up day.	they	students	plural, third person

Write the correct pronoun to complete each sentence. Choose one of the following: her, their, his, your, my, it, they.

1. Congress is the legislative branch, and _it_ is in charge of making laws.

2. If people are equal under the law, _they_ should have equal opportunities.

3. The teacher said Karana would have time later to revise _her_ paper.

4. In an absolute monarchy, the queen or king is the supreme ruler, and her or _his_ word is law.

5. The judges agree that _their_ job is to interpret the law.

6. The director said, "Joy and Tyrell, it's time to rehearse _your_ scene now."

7. Franklin stayed home and practiced _his_ speech in preparation for class.

8. I am going to take _my_ little sister to the lake for a swim.

34 | Conquer Grammar • Grade 6 • © Newmark Learning, LLC

Page 35

Name _____ Date _____

Pronoun-Antecedent Agreement

The noun that a pronoun replaces is called an antecedent. A pronoun and its antecedent must agree in number and person.

	Pronoun	Antecedent	Agreement
If **students** finish the test early, **they** can leave the room.	they	students	plural, third person
Wyatt is on the team because **he** can play well.	he	Wyatt	singular, third person

Circle the pronoun in the parentheses ( ) that correctly completes each sentence.

1. When my grandmother was younger, (you, they, **she**) had a typewriter.

2. I love going to the lake because (they, **I**, you) can relax all day.

3. If the two of us work together, (**we**, you, they) can finish cleaning today.

4. The team captains met with the principal, so (**they**, we, she) missed practice.

5. You can finish in an hour if (she, I, **you**) stay focused.

6. We took a video of the bird feeding (**its**, your, their) young.

7. The jazz band decided that (he, **they**, you) would perform next month.

8. The students study frequently so that (we, you, **they**) can get good grades.

9. I can buy milk when (she, **I**, you) go to the grocery store.

10. Jake had to go home because (**he**, you, they) needed to watch his brother.

11. The computer came with (she, **its**, we) own wireless mouse.

12. I can't go to the party because (your, they, **I**) have plans with Charlie.

Conquer Grammar • Grade 6 • © Newmark Learning, LLC | 35

Answer Key

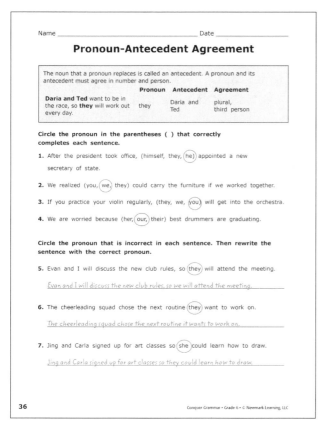

Page 36

Name _____ Date _____

Pronoun-Antecedent Agreement

The noun that a pronoun replaces is called an antecedent. A pronoun and its antecedent must agree in number and person.

	Pronoun	Antecedent	Agreement
Daria and Ted want to be in the race, so **they** will work out every day.	they	Daria and Ted	plural, third person

Circle the pronoun in the parentheses ( ) that correctly completes each sentence.

1. After the president took office, (himself, they, (he)) appointed a new secretary of state.

2. We realized (you, (we,) they) could carry the furniture if we worked together.

3. If you practice your violin regularly, (they, we, (you)) will get into the orchestra.

4. We are worried because (her, (our,) their) best drummers are graduating.

Circle the pronoun that is incorrect in each sentence. Then rewrite the sentence with the correct pronoun.

5. Evan and I will discuss the new club rules, so (they) will attend the meeting.
   Evan and I will discuss the new club rules, so we will attend the meeting.

6. The cheerleading squad chose the next routine (they) want to work on.
   The cheerleading squad chose the next routine it wants to work on.

7. Jing and Carla signed up for art classes so (she) could learn how to draw.
   Jing and Carla signed up for art classes so they could learn how to draw.

36   Conquer Grammar • Grade 6 • © Newmark Learning, LLC

Page 37

Name _____ Date _____

Pronoun-Antecedent Agreement

The noun that a pronoun replaces is called an antecedent. A pronoun and its antecedent must agree in number and person.

	Pronoun	Antecedent	Agreement
Tom went to the store. **He** bought two apples.	he	Tom	singular, third person
If **students** don't understand an assignment, **they** should ask for help.	they	students	plural, third person

Circle the pronoun in the parentheses ( ) that correctly completes each sentence.

1. The sixth grade classes met earlier about (its, (their,) they) camping trip.

2. Nate and I brought (their, he, (our)) trail map and compass for the hike.

3. The coaches doubted (his, her, (their)) decision.

4. Ariel wrote a book report about (herself, she, (her)) favorite mystery.

5. You should proofread (yourself, (your,) you) report before you turn it in.

Circle the incorrect pronoun in each sentence. Then rewrite the sentence with the correct pronoun.

6. On (its) last walk, Dan made it to the park on time for the sunrise.
   On his last walk, Dan made it to the park on time for the sunrise.

7. Delia was late for work because (her) overslept.
   Delia was late for work because she overslept.

Conquer Grammar • Grade 6 • © Newmark Learning, LLC   37

Page 38

Name _____ Date _____

Pronoun-Antecedent Agreement

The noun that a pronoun replaces is called an antecedent. A pronoun and its antecedent must agree in number and person.

	Pronoun	Antecedent	Agreement
Wendy and Lin told Dad that **they** were going to the library.	they	Wendy and Lin	plural, third person
Mr. Ruiz announced **he** will give a test tomorrow.	he	Mr. Ruiz	singular, third person

Rewrite each sentence. Replace the underlined noun or noun phrase with the correct pronoun.

1. Noami said that Noami would be here soon.
   Noami said that she would be here soon.

2. The researchers discovered some interesting documents.
   They discovered some interesting documents.

3. Julie and Alberto said the answer at the same time.
   Julie and he said the answer at the same time.

4. Why did Marc water the plant twice a day?
   Why did Marc water it twice a day?

5. The special guest read a story to the kindergarteners.
   The special guest read a story to them.

6. Tianna and I went swimming together.
   We went swimming together.

7. The director cast Gemma and Carl in the school play.
   The director cast Gemma and him in the school play.

38   Conquer Grammar • Grade 6 • © Newmark Learning, LLC

Page 39

Name _____ Date _____

Pronoun-Antecedent Agreement

The noun that a pronoun replaces is called an antecedent. A pronoun and its antecedent must agree in number and person.

	Pronoun	Antecedent	Agreement
Tessa likes to jog. **She** ran five miles yesterday.	She	Tessa	singular, third person
I waited for **Gram and Gramps**. I was excited to see **them**.	them	Gram and Gramps	plural, third person

Rewrite each sentence. Replace the underlined noun or noun phrase with the correct pronoun.

1. Emilio bought decorations for his aquarium.
   He bought decorations for his aquarium.

2. Melanie likes to sing with her sisters.
   Melanie likes to sing with them.

3. Charlotte went to the water polo match with her dad and Derek.
   Charlotte went to the water polo match with her dad and him.

4. The fans cheered and screamed for joy.
   They cheered and screamed for joy.

5. The seals swam alongside the surfers.
   The seals swam alongside them.

6. Uncle Anthony took Ricardo and me to the tournament.
   Uncle Anthony took us to the tournament.

7. My friend and I went to a Renaissance fair.
   We went to a Renaissance fair.

Conquer Grammar • Grade 6 • © Newmark Learning, LLC   39

Answer Key

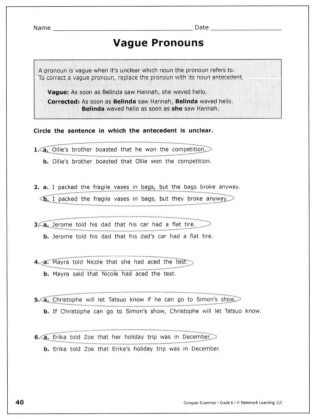

Page 40

Vague Pronouns

A pronoun is vague when it's unclear which noun the pronoun refers to. To correct a vague pronoun, replace the pronoun with its noun antecedent.

Vague: As soon as Belinda saw Hannah, she waved hello.
Corrected: As soon as Belinda saw Hannah, **Belinda** waved hello.
Belinda waved hello as soon as **she** saw Hannah.

Circle the sentence in which the antecedent is unclear.

1. a. Ollie's brother boasted that he won the competition.
   b. Ollie's brother boasted that Ollie won the competition.

2. a. I packed the fragile vases in bags, but the bags broke anyway.
   b. I packed the fragile vases in bags, but they broke anyway.

3. a. Jerome told his dad that his car had a flat tire.
   b. Jerome told his dad that his dad's car had a flat tire.

4. a. Mayra told Nicole that she had aced the test.
   b. Mayra said that Nicole had aced the test.

5. a. Christophe will let Tatsuo know if he can go to Simon's show.
   b. If Christophe can go to Simon's show, Christophe will let Tatsuo know.

6. a. Erika told Zoe that her holiday trip was in December.
   b. Erika told Zoe that Erika's holiday trip was in December.

40 — Conquer Grammar • Grade 6 • © Newmark Learning, LLC

Page 41

Vague Pronouns

A pronoun is vague when it's unclear which noun the pronoun refers to. To correct a vague pronoun, replace the pronoun with its noun antecedent.

Vague: Leo has a bike and scooter, but **it** broke.
Corrected: Leo has a bike and scooter, but **the bike** broke.
Leo has a bike and scooter, but **the scooter** broke.

In each sentence, circle the vague pronoun. Underline the two possible noun antecedents.

1. The cat chased the dog away from its favorite place on the couch.

2. Zac told Dad his shirt had a hole in it.

3. Dad drove Eric to the game after he watered the vegetable garden.

4. Maria bought a t-shirt and a dress, but it was too big for her.

Rewrite each sentence twice. Replace the vague pronoun with both possible noun antecedents.

5. I was putting my flute in the case, and I dropped it.

   a. _I was putting my flute in the case, and I dropped the case._

   b. _I was putting my flute in the case, and I dropped the flute._

6. Lia borrowed my binoculars and compass, but she forgot to return it.

   a. _Lia borrowed my binoculars and compass, but she forgot to return my binoculars._

   b. _Lia borrowed my binoculars and compass, but she forgot to return my compass._

Conquer Grammar • Grade 6 • © Newmark Learning, LLC — 41

Page 42

Vague Pronouns

A pronoun is vague when it's unclear which noun the pronoun refers to. To correct a vague pronoun, replace the pronoun with its noun antecedent.

Vague: Felix told Carey that it's **his** turn to hit the ball.
Corrected: Felix told Carey that it's **Felix's** turn to hit the ball.
Felix told Carey that it's **Carey's** turn to hit the ball.

Circle the vague pronoun or pronouns in each sentence. Then underline the two possible noun antecedents.

1. Andrea has a tablet and a cell phone, but she left it at home.

2. Ted ran into Roy when he left the theater.

3. Kim boarded the bus with Mariana after she left the office.

4. Greg told his brother that he was running too fast.

5. Amy was walking with Julia when she found a five-dollar bill.

Rewrite each sentence twice. Replace the vague pronoun with both possible noun antecedents.

6. When Yolanda forgot to return Marisol's blue sweater, she was upset.
   a. _When Yolanda forgot to return Marisol's blue sweater, Marisol was upset._

   b. _When Yolanda forgot to return Marisol's blue sweater, Yolanda was upset._

7. Rahim and Sean high-fived when he scored the winning goal.
   a. _Rahim and Sean high-fived when Rahim scored the winning goal._

   b. _Rahim and Sean high-fived when Sean scored the winning goal._

42 — Conquer Grammar • Grade 6 • © Newmark Learning, LLC

Page 43

Vague Pronouns

A pronoun is vague when it's unclear which noun the pronoun refers to. To correct a vague pronoun, replace the pronoun with its noun antecedent.

Vague: Will and Alex invited their friends to the game, but **they** got lost on the way to the stadium.
Corrected: Will and Alex invited their friends to the game, but **their friends** got lost on the way to the stadium.

Will and Alex invited their friends to the game, but **Will and Alex** got lost on the way to the stadium.

Circle the vague pronoun in each sentence. Then rewrite the sentence twice. Replace the vague pronoun with both possible noun antecedents.

1. Alba asked Raquel for help on a project after she finished her own assignment.

   a. _Alba asked Raquel for help on a project after Alba finished her own assignment._

   b. _Alba asked Raquel for help on a project after Raquel finished her own assignment._

2. As Austin added flour to the mixing bowl, he knocked it over.

   a. _As Austin added flour to the mixing bowl, he knocked the flour over._

   b. _As Austin added flour to the mixing bowl, he knocked the mixing bowl over._

3. Take the jewelry box out of the cabinet and lock it.

   a. _Take the jewelry box out of the cabinet and lock the cabinet._

   b. _Take the jewelry box out of the cabinet and lock the jewelry box._

4. My dad called Terrence after he lost his wallet.

   a. _My dad called Terrence after my dad lost his wallet._

   b. _My dad called Terrence after Terrence lost his wallet._

Conquer Grammar • Grade 6 • © Newmark Learning, LLC — 43

Answer Key

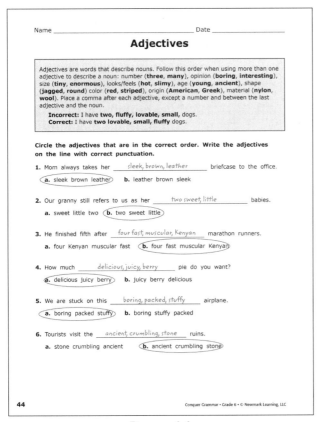

Page 44

Name _____ Date _____

Adjectives

Adjectives are words that describe nouns. Follow this order when using more than one adjective to describe a noun: number (**three, many**), opinion (**boring, interesting**), size (**tiny, enormous**), looks/feels (**hot, slimy**), age (**young, ancient**), shape (**jagged, round**) color (**red, striped**), origin (**American, Greek**), material (**nylon, wool**). Place a comma after each adjective, except a number and between the last adjective and the noun.
Incorrect: I have **two, fluffy, lovable, small, dogs.**
Correct: I have **two lovable, small, fluffy dogs.**

Circle the adjectives that are in the correct order. Write the adjectives on the line with correct punctuation.

1. Mom always takes her _sleek, brown, leather_ briefcase to the office.
   (**a. sleek brown leather**)   b. leather brown sleek

2. Our granny still refers to us as her _two sweet, little_ babies.
   a. sweet little two   (**b. two sweet little**)

3. He finished fifth after _four fast, muscular, Kenyan_ marathon runners.
   a. four Kenyan muscular fast   (**b. four fast muscular Kenyan**)

4. How much _delicious, juicy, berry_ pie do you want?
   (**a. delicious juicy berry**)   b. juicy berry delicious

5. We are stuck on this _boring, packed, stuffy_ airplane.
   (**a. boring packed stuffy**)   b. boring stuffy packed

6. Tourists visit the _ancient, crumbling, stone_ ruins.
   a. stone crumbling ancient   (**b. ancient crumbling stone**)

44   Conquer Grammar • Grade 6 • © Newmark Learning, LLC

Page 45

Name _____ Date _____

Adjectives

Adjectives are words that describe nouns. Follow this order when using more than one adjective to describe a noun: number (**thirty, some**), opinion (**clever, scary**), size (**small, massive**), looks/feels (**plump, rough**), age (**young, modern**), shape (**square, triangular**), color (**pastel, brick red**), origin (**Chinese, Peruvian**), material (**plastic, concrete**). Place a comma after each adjective, except a number and between the last adjective and the noun.
Incorrect: My dog Jericho buried **two, new, meaty, large, bones.**
Correct: My dog Jericho buried **two new, large, meaty bones.**

Write the adjectives on the line in the correct order with proper punctuation.

1. The horse ate _three long, fresh, orange_ carrots.
   (long   orange   three   fresh)

2. We hosted a _kind, tall, 15-year-old, Swedish_ exchange student.
   (15-year-old   tall   Swedish   kind)

3. I placed _several small, fragile, antique_ vases on a shelf in the closet.
   (fragile   small   antique   several)

4. Our neighbors hung _four new, different-sized, wooden_ wind chimes on their porch.
   (four   wooden   new   different-sized)

5. Luckily, I have _many friendly, 11-year-old, local_ companions.
   (local   many   11-year-old   friendly)

6. My parents attended a _funny, 2-hour-long, musical_ performance.
   (musical   2-hour-long   funny)

45   Conquer Grammar • Grade 6 • © Newmark Learning, LLC

Page 46

Name _____ Date _____

Comparative Adjectives

The comparative form of an adjective is used to compare two nouns. Follow these spelling rules to form comparative adjectives: Add -er to the end of an adjective to make it superlative. For adjectives that end in an **e**, add -r. For some adjectives that end in **y** change the **y** to **i** and then add -er. For some one-syllable adjectives, double the last consonant and add -er. If the adjective has three or more syllables, form the comparative by placing the word **more** in front of the adjective.

Adjective	Comparative Form
old	older
nice	nicer
scary	scarier
red	redder
beautiful	more beautiful

Circle the correct comparative adjective in the parentheses ( ). Then write the complete sentence on the line.

1. The cartoon before the film was actually ((**funnier**), funnyer) than the movie itself.
   The cartoon before the film was actually funnier than the movie itself.

2. The cruise ship is (bigier, (**bigger**)) than the sailboat.
   The cruise ship is bigger than the sailboat.

3. These trees are ((**greener**), more green) than those shrubs.
   These trees are greener than those shrubs.

4. Thanks to her vivid imagery, this novel is (incredibler, (**more incredible**)) than her last one.
   Thanks to her vivid imagery, this novel is more incredible than her last one.

5. Our young doctor was (capabler, (**more capable**)) and (wiseer, (**wiser**)) than we first thought.
   Our young doctor was more capable and wiser than we first thought.

46   Conquer Grammar • Grade 6 • © Newmark Learning, LLC

Page 47

Name _____ Date _____

Superlative Adjectives

The superlative form of an adjective is used to compare three or more nouns. Follow these spelling rules to form superlative adjectives: Add -est to the end of an adjective to make it superlative. For adjectives that end in **e**, simply add -st. For some adjectives that end in **y** change the **y** to **i** and then add -est. For some one-syllable adjectives, double the last consonant and add -est. If the adjective has three or more syllables, form the comparative by placing the word **most** in front of the adjective.

Adjective	Superlative Form
old	oldest
nice	nicest
scary	scariest
red	reddest
beautiful	most beautiful

Complete each sentence with the superlative form of the adjective in the parentheses ( ).

1. Do you know which climate is the _driest_?
   (dry)

2. The Hodges family live the _closest_ to our house.
   (close)

3. I cried because it was the _saddest_ movie I've ever seen.
   (sad)

4. My parents threw the _fanciest_ party when my brother graduated from college.   (fancy)

5. Study hard, because this is the _most important_ test we'll take all year!
   (important)

6. Mia has the _curliest_ hair out of all the girls on the soccer team.
   (curly)

47   Conquer Grammar • Grade 6 • © Newmark Learning, LLC

Answer Key

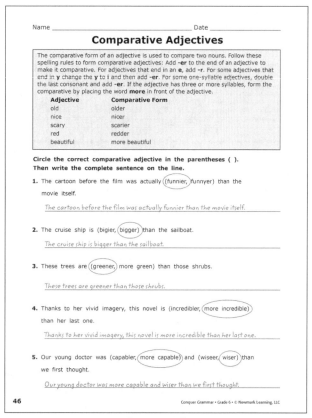

Page 48

Comparative Adjectives

The comparative form of an adjective is used to compare two nouns. Follow these spelling rules to form comparative adjectives: Add **-er** to the end of an adjective to make it comparative. For adjectives that end in an **e**, add **-r**. For some adjectives that end in **y** change the **y** to **i** and then add **-er**. For some one-syllable adjectives, double the last consonant and add **-er**. If the adjective has three or more syllables, form the comparative by placing the word **more** in front of the adjective.

Adjective	Comparative Form
old	older
nice	nicer
scary	scarier
red	redder
beautiful	more beautiful

Circle the correct comparative adjective in the parentheses ( ). Then write the complete sentence on the line.

1. The cartoon before the film was actually ((funnier,) funnyer) than the movie itself.

   The cartoon before the film was actually funnier than the movie itself.

2. The cruise ship is (bigier, (bigger)) than the sailboat.

   The cruise ship is bigger than the sailboat.

3. These trees are ((greener,) more green) than those shrubs.

   These trees are greener than those shrubs.

4. Thanks to her vivid imagery, this novel is (incredibler, (more incredible)) than her last one.

   Thanks to her vivid imagery, this novel is more incredible than her last one.

5. Our young doctor was (capabler, (more capable)) and (wiseer, (wiser)) than we first thought.

   Our young doctor was more capable and wiser than we first thought.

46

Conquer Grammar • Grade 6 • © Newmark Learning, LLC

Relative Adverbs

A relative adverb introduces a relative clause and refers to a time, a place, or a reason. The relative clause gives more information about a word or phrase in the sentence. The words **when**, **where**, and **why** may be used as relative adverbs.

Time: March is **when** the daffodils bloom.
Place: California is **where** we once lived.
Reason: I know the reason **why** the dogs were barking.

Underline the relative clause in each sentence. Circle the relative adverb.

1. Wednesday is (when) I have my singing lesson.

2. Southern France is (where) lavender grows well.

3. I'll always remember the day (when) I learned to ride a bicycle.

4. Our train conductor explained the reason (why) the train was delayed.

5. I arrived at the Grand Canyon, (where) I have been wanting to hike.

6. He did not understand the reason (why) his parents were frustrated.

7. Ethan quickly learned (why) the trail was so difficult.

8. Tomorrow is (when) I hear about my test score.

Conquer Grammar • Grade 6 • © Newmark Learning, LLC

49

Page 49

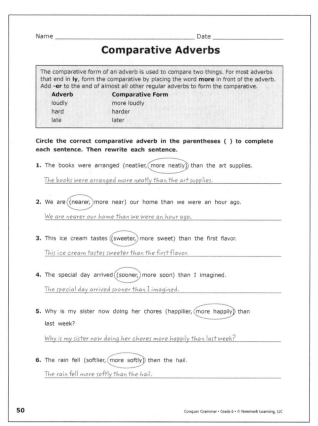

Page 50

Comparative Adverbs

The comparative form of an adverb is used to compare two things. For most adverbs that end in **ly**, form the comparative by placing the word **more** in front of the adverb. Add **-er** to the end of almost all other regular adverbs to form the comparative.

Adverb	Comparative Form
loudly	more loudly
hard	harder
late	later

Circle the correct comparative adverb in the parentheses ( ) to complete each sentence. Then rewrite each sentence.

1. The books were arranged (neatlier, (more neatly)) than the art supplies.

   The books were arranged more neatly than the art supplies.

2. We are ((nearer,) more near) our home than we were an hour ago.

   We are nearer our home than we were an hour ago.

3. This ice cream tastes ((sweeter,) more sweet) than the first flavor.

   This ice cream tastes sweeter than the first flavor.

4. The special day arrived ((sooner,) more soon) than I imagined.

   The special day arrived sooner than I imagined.

5. Why is my sister now doing her chores (happilier, (more happily)) than last week?

   Why is my sister now doing her chores more happily than last week?

6. The rain fell (softlier, (more softly)) than the hail.

   The rain fell more softly than the hail.

50

Conquer Grammar • Grade 6 • © Newmark Learning, LLC

Superlative Adverbs

The superlative form of an adverb is used to compare three or more things. For most adverbs that end in **ly**, form the comparative by placing the word **most** in front of the adverb. Add **-est** to the end of almost all other regular adverbs to form the superlative.

Adverb	Superlative Form
loudly	most loudly
hard	hardest
late	latest

Complete each sentence with the superlative form of the adverb in the parentheses ( ).

1. The sun shines the ___most brightly___ of all the stars in the sky.
   (brightly)

2. Six o'clock in the evening is the ___soonest___ I can be home for dinner.
   (soon)

3. Who is the ___fastest___ swimmer on the team?
   (fast)

4. We all agree that my sister sings the ___most sweetly___.
   (sweetly)

5. Miss Ford is the ___kindest___ of all the teachers at our school.
   (kind)

6. I see the ___most clearly___ when I wear my eyeglasses.
   (clearly)

7. Today was the ___coldest___ day of the year.
   (cold)

Conquer Grammar • Grade 6 • © Newmark Learning, LLC

51

Page 51

Answer Key

Name _____ Date _____

Prepositions

A preposition shows the relationship between a noun or pronoun and another word in the sentence. The relationship may show **what**, **when**, **where**, or **how**. Some common prepositions include **about, above, across, after, against, around, at, before, behind, below, beside, between, by, during, for, from, in, near, of, on, out, over, through, to, toward, under, until, up, with.**

We sat **under** a shady tree and listened **to** music **for** an hour.
My service dog came **with** us.

Circle each preposition and underline the noun or noun phrase that relates to the preposition.

1. Luckily, my favorite park is (near) my house.

2. You can see many colorful birds (in) the trees.

3. Someday, I want to row a boat (across) the lake.

4. I often ride my bicycle (around) the perimeter.

5. There will be many concerts (at) the stadium.

6. We try to go (with) our friends when we can.

7. There are fireflies glowing (by) the bushes.

8. The dogs sat (under) the table.

9. Put your umbrella (beside) the door.

10. My sister and I walked (toward) the lake.

52   Conquer Grammar • Grade 6 • © Newmark Learning, LLC

Page 52

Name _____ Date _____

Prepositions

A preposition shows the relationship between a noun or pronoun and another word in the sentence. The relationship may show **what**, **when**, **where**, or **how**. Some common prepositions include **about, above, across, after, against, around, at, before, behind, below, beside, between, by, during, for, from, in, near, of, on, out, over, through, to, toward, under, until, up, with.**

The boys ran **through** the narrow hallway.

Write a preposition or prepositions to complete each sentence.
Possible answers are provided.

1. The ferry took us _____to_____ the island.

2. We traveled _____across_____ the ocean's choppy water.

3. The journey took _____between_____ twenty and twenty-five minutes.

4. I forgot to check my watch _____before_____ we left the shore.

5. We walked _____from_____ the dock _____toward_____ the town.

6. After wandering _____through_____ charming streets, we found a place _____to_____ rest.

7. _____During_____ our brief visit, we only got an overview _____of_____ this lovely place.

8. The kitten hid _____between_____ the boxes.

53   Conquer Grammar • Grade 6 • © Newmark Learning, LLC

Page 53

Name _____ Date _____

Correlative Conjunctions

Correlative conjunctions always come in pairs and appear in different parts of a sentence. They work together to connect the parts of the sentence.
Use the correlative conjunctions **both . . . and** to add one idea to another.
Either . . . or gives an alternative. **Neither . . . nor** gives no alternative.
Not only . . . but also contrasts two ideas.

Both Michelle **and** Bonnie want to learn a new language.
They will choose **either** Spanish **or** French.
Neither Italian **nor** German is offered at their school.
Learning another language is **not only** challenging **but also** rewarding.

Join each pair of sentences with the correlative conjunctions in the parentheses ( ). Write the sentence on the line.

1. At the farm, there was an apple orchard. There was also a pumpkin patch.
   (both . . . and)
   At the farm, there was both an apple orchard and a pumpkin patch.

2. We can buy an apple pie. We can buy a pumpkin pie.
   (either . . . or)
   We can buy either an apple pie or a pumpkin pie.

3. Ice cream is good on pie. Whipped cream is tasty on it, too.
   (not only . . . but also)
   Pie is not only good with ice cream, but also tasty with whipped cream.

4. The pumpkin was too heavy. My brother and I couldn't lift it.
   (neither . . . nor)
   Neither my brother nor I could lift the heavy pumpkin.

5. My brother wants to be a farmer. So do I.
   (both . . . and)
   Both my brother and I want to be farmers.

54   Conquer Grammar • Grade 6 • © Newmark Learning, LLC

Page 54

Name _____ Date _____

Nonrestrictive Clauses

Nonrestrictive clauses are not essential to the meaning of a sentence. A nonrestrictive clause can be deleted without changing the sentence's meaning. Nonrestrictive clauses are usually set off from the rest of the sentence with commas, dashes, or parentheses.

The novels, **which are my favorites**, are now movies, too.
The novels **(which are my favorites)** are now movies, too.
The novels—**which are my favorites**—are now movies, too.

Rewrite each sentence. Use the punctuation named in the parentheses ( ) to set off the nonrestrictive clause.

1. Alonzo who is a little shy isn't sure he wants to audition for the play. (commas)
   Alonzo, who is a little shy, isn't sure he wants to audition for the play.

2. I hope though I am doubtful that he'll change his mind. (parentheses)
   I hope (though I am doubtful) that he'll change his mind.

3. Dory and Ray both terrific artists are working on the scenery. (dashes)
   Dory and Ray—both terrific artists—are working on the scenery.

4. Josh who is very funny is writing a comedy sketch. (commas)
   Josh, who is very funny, is writing a comedy sketch.

5. The materials which I still need to buy are on sale. (commas)
   The materials, which I still need to buy, are on sale.

6. My aunt who sews her own clothes will help with the costumes. (dashes)
   My aunt—who sews her own clothes—will help with the costumes.

55   Conquer Grammar • Grade 6 • © Newmark Learning, LLC

Page 55

Answer Key

Name _____ Date _____

Nonrestrictive Clauses

Nonrestrictive clauses are not essential to the meaning of a sentence. A nonrestrictive clause can be deleted without changing the sentence's meaning. Nonrestrictive clauses are usually set off from the rest of the sentence with commas, dashes, or parentheses.

Curtis, **who won the blue ribbon for his illustration,** is my cousin.
Two of my classmates **(Val and Chiara)** made the team.
The Lightning Thief—**the best book ever!**—is about twelve-year-old Percy Jackson.

Rewrite each sentence. Use the punctuation named in the parentheses ( ) to set off the nonrestrictive clause.

1. T.J. the boy who aced the geometry test is my brother. (parentheses)
   T.J. (the boy who aced the geometry test) is my brother.

2. We Shelli and Kiara raced to the finish line. (dashes)
   We—Shelli and Kiara—raced to the finish line.

3. My mother who is a police officer is going to speak about safety. (commas)
   My mother, who is a police officer, is going to speak about safety.

4. My bicycle which is in the garage needs new brakes. (parentheses)
   My bicycle (which is in the garage) needs new brakes.

5. A great song my favorite one in the whole world! just came on the radio. (dashes)
   A great song—my favorite one in the whole world!—just came on the radio.

6. Ricky who is the smartest boy I know wants to be a professor someday. (commas)
   Ricky, who is the smartest boy I know, wants to be a professor someday.

Page 56

Name _____ Date _____

Nonrestrictive Clauses

Nonrestrictive clauses are not essential to the meaning of a sentence. A nonrestrictive clause can be deleted without changing the sentence's meaning. Nonrestrictive clauses are usually set off from the rest of the sentence with commas, dashes, or parentheses.

Cole, **who sits next to me in Spanish class,** is my best friend.
Both of my favorite teams **(San Antonio and Cleveland)** are in the finals!
Holes—**my favorite book**—was made into a movie.

Rewrite each sentence. Use the punctuation named in the parentheses ( ) to set off the nonrestrictive clause.

1. Kendall who is class president is absent today. (commas)
   Kendall, who is class president, is absent today.

2. Lulu wants to visit all three cities London, Rome, and Shanghai. (parentheses)
   Lulu wants to visit all three cities (London, Rome, and Shanghai).

3. The toddlers who are really energetic ran around in the yard. (dashes)
   The toddlers—who are really energetic—ran around in the yard.

4. We Paco, Jessie, and I decided to go to the library today. (parentheses)
   We (Paco, Jessie, and I) decided to go to the library today.

5. Three students Aldo, Ricky, and Jen volunteered to help. (dashes)
   Three students—Aldo, Ricky, and Jen—volunteered to help.

6. I painted my bike red my favorite color, but it's not dry yet. (parentheses)
   I painted my bike red (my favorite color), but it's not dry yet.

7. I like to eat grapes sour or sweet with cheese. (parentheses)
   I like to eat grapes (sour or sweet) with cheese.

Page 57

Name _____ Date _____

Nonrestrictive Clauses

Nonrestrictive clauses are not essential to the meaning of a sentence. A nonrestrictive clause can be deleted without changing the sentence's meaning. Nonrestrictive clauses are usually set off from the rest of the sentence with commas, dashes, or parentheses.

Mr. Green, **who lives next door,** works at the art supply store.

Rewrite each sentence. Use the punctuation named in the parentheses ( ) to set off the nonrestrictive clause.

1. Victoria asked Carly who's in her class if she could borrow a pencil. (commas)
   Victoria asked Carly, who's in her class, if she could borrow a pencil.

2. The two friends Tory and Sarah Jane are writing a song. (parentheses)
   The two friends (Tory and Sarah Jane) are writing a song.

3. That shot Malcolm made that last one was incredible! (dashes)
   That shot Malcolm made—that last one—was incredible!

4. The note which was written in code told me where to go. (commas)
   The note, which was written in code, told me where to go.

5. Mara who is my best friend lives in Oregon. (parentheses)
   Mara (who is my best friend) lives in Oregon.

6. To train for the race which I want to win I cycle five miles a day. (commas)
   To train for the race, which I want to win, I cycle five miles a day.

7. Ralph found all of Ariel's e-mail addresses two in total in the directory. (dashes)
   Ralph found all of Ariel's e-mail addresses—two in total—in the directory.

Page 58

Name _____ Date _____

Nonrestrictive and Restrictive Clauses

A nonrestrictive clause is not essential to a sentence's meaning. Nonrestrictive clauses are set off from the rest of the sentence with commas, dashes, or parentheses.

My neighbor, **whom I admire,** is a veterinarian.
My neighbor **(whom I admire)** is a veterinarian.
My neighbor—**whom I admire**—is a veterinarian.

A restrictive clause is essential to a sentence's meaning, and should not be set off from the rest of the sentence.

The genre **that I like best** is science fiction.

If the underlined clause is restrictive, write R. If it is nonrestrictive, write N and add commas where needed.

1. Our school will be closed on Thanksgiving, which is my favorite holiday. ___N___

2. Sanjay loves any book that is about Greek or Roman mythology. ___R___

3. The actor, who is in my favorite movie, will be at the mall on Saturday. ___N___

4. Jeremiah, the boy we met last week, will be at the pool party. ___N___

Rewrite each sentence. Use the punctuation named in the parentheses ( ) to set off the nonrestrictive clause.

5. North Street as seen on the map is near Fairview Avenue. (parentheses)
   North Street (as seen on the map) is near Fairview Avenue.

6. The tuba I know it's big is the instrument I'm learning to play. (dashes)
   The tuba—I know it's big—is the instrument I'm learning to play.

7. The glee club which rehearses daily will perform on Friday. (commas)
   The glee club, which rehearses daily, will perform on Friday.

Page 59

Answer Key

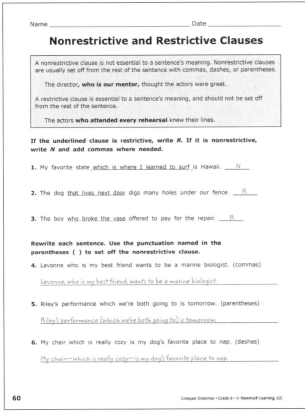

Page 60

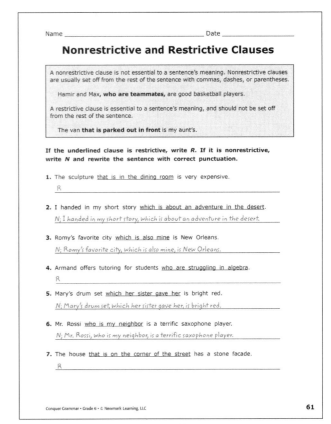

Page 61

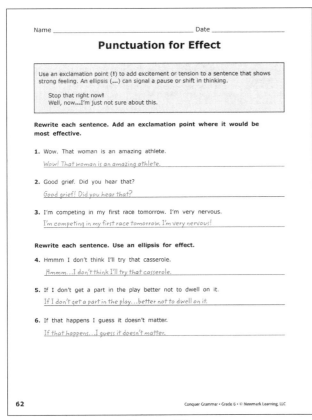

Page 62

Punctuation for Effect

Use an exclamation point (!) to add excitement or tension to a sentence that shows strong feeling. An ellipsis (...) can signal a pause or shift in thinking.

No way! I'm not any good at acting...or maybe I am.

Rewrite each sentence. Add an exclamation point or an ellipsis where it would be most effective.

1. It started to snow after the first inning. I just couldn't believe it.
   It started to snow after the first inning. I just couldn't believe it!

2. I'm staying home, and that's final.
   I'm staying home, and that's final!

3. I'd like to go. I'm just concerned that I won't know anyone there.
   I'd like to go...I'm just concerned that I won't know anyone there.

4. Well I wish you'd reconsider.
   Well...I wish you'd reconsider.

5. I turned the corner and saw it. A turkey stood right on Oak Lane.
   I turned the corner and saw it...a turkey stood right on Oak Lane!

6. Oh, no. I've lost my library book.
   Oh, no! I've lost my library book.

7. We wonder what would have occurred. Oh well, we'll never know now.
   We wonder what would have occurred...oh well, we'll never know now.

Page 63

105

Answer Key

Name _____ Date _____

Capitalization in Dialogue

Dialogue is a conversation between two or more people or characters. Quotation marks set off a speaker's exact words. Always capitalize the first word in the quotation marks. If the dialogue is interrupted, do not capitalize the first word in the continuation of the dialogue unless the speaker's tag ends in a period.

"Let's meet at my house today," said my best friend.
Peter said, "You have a dentist appointment tomorrow."
"Let's meet at my house," Lucy said, "so we can walk to the station."

Rewrite each sentence with correct capitalization.

1. Mr. Peterson announced, "your research papers were all very impressive."

   Mr. Peterson announced, "Your research papers were all very impressive."

2. "what are your plans for the weekend?" asked Irma.

   "What are your plans for the weekend?" asked Irma.

3. "my plans involve studying," I said. "they will also include basketball."

   "My plans involve studying," I said. "They will also include basketball."

4. Irma inquired, "would you like to shoot some hoops with my brother and me?"

   Irma inquired, "Would you like to shoot some hoops with my brother and me?"

5. "sure, but could we meet on Sunday?" I answered.

   "Sure, but could we meet on Sunday?" I answered.

6. "if I get all my work done on Saturday, I'll have much more fun," I promised.

   "If I get all my work done on Saturday, I'll have much more fun," I promised.

7. "so, Sunday it is," said Irma, "And we can meet at my house."

   "So, Sunday it is," said Irma, "and we can meet at my house."

64   Conquer Grammar • Grade 6 • © Newmark Learning, LLC

Page 64

Name _____ Date _____

Capitalization and Punctuation in Titles

Capitalize the first and last word and each additional main word of a book or song title. Unless it is the first or last word of the title, do not capitalize **a**, **an**, and **the**, or most short prepositions, such as **at**, **in**, **by**, **for**, **of**, and **to**. Always underline a book, movie, or magazine title and place an article, poem, song, or story title in quotation marks.

Book title: A Wrinkle in Time
Song title: "America the Beautiful"

Rewrite each sentence with correct capitalization. Be sure to underline the book titles and put quotation marks around the song titles.

1. I am reading the book, math and music, to find out how the topics are similar.

   I am reading the book, Math and Music, to find out how the topics are similar.

2. I liked reading little women, but my brother preferred the call of the wild.

   I liked reading Little Women, but my brother preferred The Call of the Wild.

3. The patriotic song, you're a grand old flag, is very catchy.

   The patriotic song, "You're a Grand Old Flag," is very catchy.

4. I just finished reading about a vet in the book, all creatures great and small.

   I just finished reading about a vet in the book, All Creatures Great and Small.

5. The first song I can remember singing is twinkle, twinkle, little star.

   The first song I can remember singing is "Twinkle, Twinkle, Little Star."

6. My father's favorite mystery novel is the hound of the baskervilles.

   My father's favorite mystery novel is The Hound of the Baskervilles.

Conquer Grammar • Grade 6 • © Newmark Learning, LLC   65

Page 65

Name _____ Date _____

Capitalization and Punctuation in Titles

Capitalize the first and last word and each additional main word of a book or song title. Unless it is the first or last word of the title, do not capitalize **a**, **an**, and **the**, or most short prepositions, such as **at**, **in**, **by**, **for**, **of**, and **to**. Always underline a book, movie, play, or magazine title and place an article, poem, song, or story title in quotation marks.

Book title: The Odyssey
Article title: "The Scientist"

Underline the title in each sentence. Then rewrite the sentence with correct punctuation and capitalization.

1. I borrowed a copy of national geographic from the magazine rack.

   I borrowed a copy of National Geographic from the magazine rack.

2. Have you seen the movie where the red fern grows, based on the book?

   Have you seen the movie Where the Red Fern Grows, based on the book?

3. My parents read the new york times every Sunday.

   My parents read The New York Times every Sunday.

4. Shakespeare's romeo and juliet is a play most people are familiar with.

   Shakespeare's Romeo and Juliet is a play most people are familiar with.

5. I bought biking around paris to take on our trip.

   I bought Biking Around Paris to take on our trip.

6. My sister loved the classic movie she saw last weekend, the sound of music.

   My sister loved the classic movie she saw last weekend, The Sound of Music.

66   Conquer Grammar • Grade 6 • © Newmark Learning, LLC

Page 66

Name _____ Date _____

Capitalization and Punctuation in Titles

Capitalize the first and last word and each additional main word of a book or song title. Unless it is the first or last word of the title, do not capitalize **a**, **an**, and **the**, or most short prepositions, such as **at**, **in**, **by**, **for**, **of**, and **to**. Always underline a book, movie, or magazine title and place an article, poem, song, or story title in quotation marks.

Rewrite each sentence with correct capitalization and punctuation for the titles.

1. I just finished a great article, the secret world of icebergs.

   I just finished a great article, "The Secret World of Icebergs."

2. I am trying to memorize paul revere's ride, a poem by
   Henry Wadsworth Longfellow.

   I am trying to memorize "Paul Revere's Ride," a poem by

   Henry Wadsworth Longfellow.

3. I liked Poe's short story, the black cat, but my brother preferred
   the tell-tale heart.

   I liked Poe's short story, "The Black Cat," but my brother preferred

   "The Tell-Tale Heart."

4. May I teach you the song I learned at summer camp, on top of spaghetti?

   May I teach you the song I learned at summer camp, "On Top of Spaghetti"?

5. My mother's favorite short story is the legend of sleepy hollow.

   My mother's favorite short story is "The Legend of Sleepy Hollow."

Conquer Grammar • Grade 6 • © Newmark Learning, LLC   67

Page 67

Answer Key

Name _____ Date _____

Sentence Fragments

A sentence fragment is an incomplete sentence that does not express a complete thought. It is missing a subject, a verb, or both. To correct a fragment, add the missing subject or verb.

Fragment: Ran the race in record time.
Complete sentence: Lizzy ran the race in record time.
Fragment: The crowd for her achievement.
Complete sentence: The crowd **cheered** for her achievement.

Determine which of the two choices is a fragment and which is a complete sentence. Circle the fragment.

1. a. The community center across the road from the school. *(circled)*
   b. The community center is right across the road from the school.

2. a. The two girls studied for their history test next week.
   b. Studied for the history test next week. *(circled)*

3. a. We should have enough games and activities for the party at Rivington Park.
   b. Enough games and activities for the party at Rivington Park. *(circled)*

Rewrite each fragment as a complete sentence. Circle the word in the parentheses ( ) that corrects the fragment. Then write the complete sentence on the line.

4. The team to the field after the rain delay. (players, *returned*)
   The team returned to the field after the rain delay.

5. The announced that a prize had been awarded. (*judge*, earlier)
   The judge announced that a prize had been awarded.

6. The badminton players in the gym. (coach, *practiced*)
   The badminton players practiced in the gym.

Page 68

Name _____ Date _____

Run-On Sentences

A run-on sentence contains two or more complete thoughts. One way to correct a run-on sentence is to separate it into two or more complete sentences, each with a subject and a verb. Another way is to add a comma between the complete thoughts and a coordinating conjunction such as **and, but, or,** or **so.**

Run-On: April went to the store after school she bought a yogurt.
Corrected: April went to the store after school. **S**he bought a yogurt.
April went to the store after school, **and** she bought a yogurt.

Rewrite each run-on sentence as two or more complete sentences.

1. Did Dawn research whales online did she find enough information?
   Did Dawn research whales online? Did she find enough information?

2. If she likes animals, she should study zoology she should study biology, too.
   If she likes animals, she should study zoology. She should study biology, too.

3. Marianne was absent for three days she is behind in her group project.
   Marianne was absent for three days. She is behind in her group project.

4. I can't believe that he didn't hear the thunder it was so loud!
   I can't believe that he didn't hear the thunder. It was so loud!

5. Have you finished I think it's finally my turn.
   Have you finished? I think it's finally my turn.

6. I can't believe it that is an amazing story!
   I can't believe it. That is an amazing story!

7. We went for a walk in the woods and saw some unusual birds, which I loved, then we went to get lunch, which I thought was pretty tasty, it was a delightful day.
   We went for a walk in the woods and saw some unusual birds, which
   I loved. Then we went to get lunch, which I thought was pretty
   tasty. It was a delightful day.

Page 69

Name _____ Date _____

Run-On Sentences

A run-on sentence contains two or more complete thoughts. One way to correct a run-on sentence is to separate it into two or more complete sentences, each with a subject and a verb. Another way is to add a comma between the complete thoughts and a coordinating conjunction such as **and, but, or,** or **so.**

Run-On: My father knew I was exhausted he let me sleep.
Corrected: My father knew I was exhausted. **H**e let me sleep.
My father knew I was exhausted, **so** he let me sleep.

Correct each run-on sentence. Use a comma and the conjunction in the parentheses ( ). Write the new sentence on the line.

1. Jada is on the track team Christa is on the volleyball team. (and)
   Jada is on the track team, and Christa is on the volleyball team.

2. Cesar likes algebra Jean-Pierre prefers language arts. (but)
   Cesar likes algebra, but Jean-Pierre prefers language arts.

3. Serena placed first in the state she is going to the nationals. (so)
   Serena placed first in the state, so she is going to the nationals.

4. We could order sushi for lunch we could get pizza. (or)
   We could order sushi for lunch, or we could get pizza.

5. Eli wanted to ride the roller coaster he's too little. (but)
   Eli wanted to ride the roller coaster, but he's too little.

6. I want to ace the next exam I'm going to study for an hour every night. (so)
   I want to ace the next exam, so I'm going to study for an hour every night.

7. Lucas went to a movie in the morning he saw a play in the evening. (and)
   Lucas went to a movie in the morning, and he saw a play in the evening.

Page 70

Name _____ Date _____

Run-On Sentences

A run-on sentence contains two or more complete thoughts. One way to correct a run-on sentence is to separate it into two or more complete sentences, each with a subject and a verb. Another way is to add a comma between the complete thoughts and a coordinating conjunction such as **and, but, or,** or **so.**

Run-On: We've had so much rain they say it's good for the plants.
Corrected: We've had so much rain. They say it's good for the plants.
We've had so much rain, **but** they say it's good for the plants.

Rewrite each run-on sentence as two complete sentences.

1. It is nearly four o'clock the ferry will already have left.
   It is nearly four o'clock. The ferry will already have left.

2. Marguerite practices her piccolo every day she adores music.
   Marguerite practices her piccolo every day. She adores music.

3. Have you finished reading that chapter yet can you go outside now?
   Have you finished reading that chapter yet? Can you go outside now?

Correct each run-on sentence. Use a comma and the conjunction in the parentheses ( ). Write the new sentence on the line.

4. Kenneth is my brother Kenny is his nickname. (and)
   Kenneth is my brother, and Kenny is his nickname.

5. It's Sunday the library is closed. (so)
   It's Sunday, so the library is closed.

6. Carter loved the movie Rafael preferred the book. (but)
   Carter loved the movie, but Rafael preferred the book.

Page 71

Answer Key

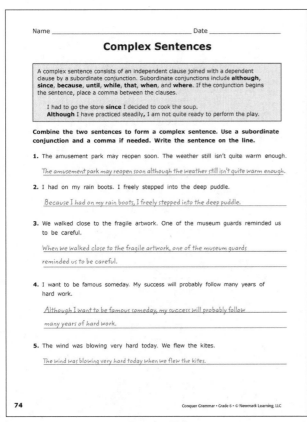

Page 72

Name _____ Date _____

Sentence Fragments and Run-On Sentences

A sentence fragment does not express a complete thought. It is missing a subject, a verb, or both. To correct a fragment, add the missing subject or verb. A run-on sentence consists of two or more complete thoughts. One way to correct a run-on sentence is to divide it into two or more complete sentences. Another way is to add a comma between the complete thoughts and a coordinating conjunction such as **and**, **but**, **or**, or **so**.

Fragment: Runs with her dog whenever the weather is nice.
Corrected: Yolanda runs with her dog whenever the weather is nice.

Run-On: Harry brought an extra bottle of juice he was sure he'd be thirsty.
Corrected: Harry brought an extra bottle of juice. **He** was sure he'd be thirsty.

Rewrite each run-on sentence as two complete sentences.

1. The queen appointed the ministers they were her most trusted advisors.

   The queen appointed the ministers. They were her most trusted advisors.

2. Anna was a respected queen she reigned for decades.

   Anna was a respected queen. She reigned for decades.

3. We saw the coronation on TV it was spectacular!

   We saw the coronation on TV. It was spectacular!

Circle the word or phrase in the parentheses ( ) that corrects the fragment. Then write each fragment as a complete sentence.

4. Voted for the bill. (⟨The ministers⟩ Last week)

   The ministers voted for the bill.

5. As the ball sailed through the goalpost! (The crowd, ⟨Fans cheered⟩)

   Fans cheered as the ball sailed through the goalpost!

6. Studying for the spelling quiz? (⟨Are you,⟩ Why)

   Are you studying for the spelling quiz?

72   Conquer Grammar • Grade 6 • © Newmark Learning, LLC

Page 73

Name _____ Date _____

Complex Sentences

A complex sentence consists of an independent clause joined with a dependent clause by a subordinate conjunction. Subordinate conjunctions include **although**, **since**, **because**, **until**, **while**, **that**, **when**, and **where**. If the conjunction begins the sentence, place a comma between the clauses.

I kept reading the short story **until** I finished it.
Although I have practiced steadily, I am not yet ready for the piano recital.

Draw one line under the independent clause in each sentence. Draw two lines under the dependent clause.

1. The little girl laughed because her big brother made a funny face.

2. When our alarm didn't go off, my sister and I overslept.

3. The birds soared above the lake while the giraffes drank from it.

4. Although the day was hot, there was a refreshing breeze.

Combine each pair of sentences to form a complex sentence. Use a subordinate conjunction and a comma if needed. Write the sentence on the line.

5. Honey bees are considered social insects. They work together for survival.

   Because they work together for survival, honey bees are considered social insects.

6. These bees live in a hive. They are very industrious.

   These bees live in a hive where they are very industrious.

Conquer Grammar • Grade 6 • © Newmark Learning, LLC   73

Page 74

Name _____ Date _____

Complex Sentences

A complex sentence consists of an independent clause joined with a dependent clause by a subordinate conjunction. Subordinate conjunctions include **although**, **since**, **because**, **until**, **while**, **that**, **when**, and **where**. If the conjunction begins the sentence, place a comma between the clauses.

I had to go the store **since** I decided to cook the soup.
Although I have practiced steadily, I am not quite ready to perform the play.

Combine the two sentences to form a complex sentence. Use a subordinate conjunction and a comma if needed. Write the sentence on the line.

1. The amusement park may reopen soon. The weather still isn't quite warm enough.

   The amusement park may reopen soon although the weather still isn't quite warm enough.

2. I had on my rain boots. I freely stepped into the deep puddle.

   Because I had on my rain boots, I freely stepped into the deep puddle.

3. We walked close to the fragile artwork. One of the museum guards reminded us to be careful.

   When we walked close to the fragile artwork, one of the museum guards reminded us to be careful.

4. I want to be famous someday. My success will probably follow many years of hard work.

   Although I want to be famous someday, my success will probably follow many years of hard work.

5. The wind was blowing very hard today. We flew the kites.

   The wind was blowing very hard today when we flew the kites.

74   Conquer Grammar • Grade 6 • © Newmark Learning, LLC

Page 75

Name _____ Date _____

Reducing Sentences

Writers often reduce sentences by deleting words and phrases that are unnecessary or not important. Reducing sentences helps make writing clearer.

To relax, we listened to some soothing music ~~but I'm not sure who the artist is~~.
When I was 7 years old ~~or maybe 7 and a half~~, I lost my first tooth.

Rewrite each sentence. Delete any unnecessary or unimportant information.

1. My teacher, who is named Mrs. Greene just like my neighbor, read a wonderful story to the class.

   My teacher, Mrs. Greene, read a wonderful story to the class.

2. The new song I just heard on the radio that sounded like another song whose name I can't remember is really upbeat.

   The new song I just heard on the radio is really upbeat.

3. Whenever it's time to harvest my vegetable garden, I'm surprised to see how much the deer have eaten, and I see those deer all around my neighborhood.

   Whenever it's time to harvest my vegetable garden, I'm surprised to see how much the deer have eaten.

4. I liked how fresh the grass smelled in the foggy morning air, even though some of the grass was green and some of it was brown.

   I liked how fresh the grass smelled in the foggy morning air.

5. I saw Mr. Hodge's car window was open and I heard emergency warnings going off because a dangerous storm was about to hit our town.

   I heard emergency warnings going off because a dangerous storm was about to hit our town.

Conquer Grammar • Grade 6 • © Newmark Learning, LLC   75

Answer Key

Name _____ Date _____

Varying Sentence Patterns

Skilled writers use a variety of sentence types to create interest and avoid choppy writing. One way to vary sentences is by combining related sentences using a comma and a conjunction such as **and**, **but**, **or**, **so**, or **yet**.

Steph bought a watch, **and** I did, too.
Angie bought a vest, **but** she didn't get anything else.
Amir can buy a new tie, **or** he can borrow his dad's.
Myra bought mittens, **so** her hands are no longer cold.
Yoshi liked the jacket, **yet** he chose not to buy it.

Rewrite each pair of sentences as one complete sentence. Use a comma and the conjunction in the parentheses ( ).

1. Ebony swam across the pool. Her brother timed her.   (and)
   Ebony swam across the pool, and her brother timed her.

2. The boys complained about the drizzle. They continued to play soccer.   (yet)
   The boys complained about the drizzle, yet they continued to play soccer.

3. My sister is right-handed. I am left-handed.   (but)
   My sister is right-handed, but I am left-handed.

4. We could see a ballet. We could go to the opera.   (or)
   We could see a ballet, or we could go to the opera.

5. The mail carrier crossed the street. She avoided the barking dog.   (so)
   The mail carrier crossed the street, so she avoided the barking dog.

6. Bella ate an orange. I ate a bowl of cherries.   (and)
   Bella ate an orange, and I ate a bowl of cherries.

7. Lana entered the store. She bought shoes.   (and)
   Lana entered the store, and she bought shoes.

76
Conquer Grammar • Grade 6 • © Newmark Learning, LLC

Page 76

Name _____ Date _____

Varying Sentence Patterns

Skilled writers use a variety of sentence types to create interest and avoid choppy writing. One way to vary sentences is by combining related sentences using a comma and a conjunction such as **and**, **but**, **or**, **so**, or **yet**. You may also use the conjunction **and** or **or** to join the subjects (if the predicate appears in both sentences) or predicates (if the subject appears in both sentences) of two sentences.

Jasmine walked to the store, **but** it was closed.
Jasmine **and** Frida walked to the store.

Rewrite each sentence. Use a conjunction to combine the two sentences. Be sure to add a comma if needed.

Possible answers are provided.

1. Last weekend, my mom and I went to our neighbor's house. Mom and I went to see her new puppies.
   Last weekend, my mom and I went to our neighbor's house so we could see her new puppies.

2. My mom let me pick out a puppy. I took her home.
   My mom let me pick out a puppy, and I took her home.

3. We bought some toys for the new puppy. We set up a dog bed, too.
   We bought some toys and we set up a dog bed for the new puppy.

4. I got the puppy yesterday. She can't stop wagging her tail.
   I got the puppy yesterday, and she can't stop wagging her tail.

5. My friend Roberto likes to snowboard. I like to snowboard, too.
   My friend Roberto and I like to snowboard.

6. The snow is cold. Our special gear keeps us warm.
   The snow is cold, but our special gear keeps us warm.

Conquer Grammar • Grade 6 • © Newmark Learning, LLC
77

Page 77

Name _____ Date _____

Varying Sentence Patterns

There are several ways to vary sentence patterns. You can combine related sentences with a conjunction such as **after**, **although**, **because**, **before**, **if**, **since**, **when**, **while**, or **unless**. You can also switch the order of the words in a sentence, beginning the sentence with a conjunction. Always place a comma after the phrase introduced by the conjunction.

I studied hard **because** I wanted to do well in school.
Because I wanted to do well in school, I studied hard.

Rewrite each paragraph. Combine sentences and begin sentences with one of the following conjunctions: after, although, because, before, if, since, when, while, unless.

Possible answers are provided.

1. The Grand Canyon attracts millions of visitors each year. It is considered one of the seven natural wonders of the world. You can view the canyon from either the North Rim or the South Rim. Both sides are breathtaking. The South Rim attracts more visitors. The South Rim is easily accessible.
   Because it is considered one of the seven natural wonders of the world, the Grand Canyon attracts millions of visitors each year. You can view the canyon from either the North Rim or the South Rim. Although both sides are breathtaking, the South Rim attracts more visitors since it is easily accessible.

2. You go outside at night. You can see the moon. Have you ever wondered why? The moon does not give off any light of its own. It appears very bright in the evening sky. We are able to see the moon. Sunlight reflects off its surface and into our eyes.
   When you go outside at night, have you ever wondered why you can see the moon? Although the moon appears very bright in the evening sky, it does not give off any light of its own. We are able to see the moon because sunlight reflects off its surface and into our eyes.

78
Conquer Grammar • Grade 6 • © Newmark Learning, LLC

Page 78

Name _____ Date _____

Homophones

Homophones are words that sound the same but have different spellings and meanings. Some examples of homophones include **son/sun**, **made/maid**, and **heard/herd**.

Talking is not **allowed** during the show.   **Allowed** means "permitted."
Therefore, nobody spoke **aloud**.   **Aloud** means "able to be heard."

Circle the two words that sound the same in each sentence. Then write the word that matches the definition.

1. "How Bear Lost Its (Tail)" is my favorite (tale).
   Story is another word for ___tale___.

2. It is a (principle) of our school (principal) to know each student's name.
   A ___principle___ is "a rule of conduct."

3. The completion of the work at the construction (site) is a welcome (sight).
   Location is another word for ___site___.

4. (Would) you prefer a door made of (wood) or metal?
   Lumber is another word for ___wood___.

5. I finished my algebra (lesson) on Friday to (lessen) my homework on Saturday.
   Reduce is another word for ___lessen___.

6. (Whether) we go snorkeling today or tomorrow depends on the (weather).
   If is another word for ___whether___.

7. In an incredible (feat) of strength, Calvin sprinted the last hundred (feet).
   Achievement is another word for ___feat___.

Conquer Grammar • Grade 6 • © Newmark Learning, LLC
79

Page 79

Answer Key

Page 80

Homophones

Homophones are words that sound the same but have different spellings and meanings. Some examples of homophones include to/two/too, there/their/they're, and **passed/past**.

Whether or not we have the picnic depends on the **weather**.

Circle the two words that sound the same in each sentence. Then write the word that matches the definition.

1. I can't practice my new (piece) unless I have (peace) and quiet.
   Calm is another word for _____peace_____.

2. (There) is no way we can play baseball in (their) small backyard.
   _____Their_____ is a **pronoun**.

3. The parade always (passed) by our grandparents' house in (past) years.
   Previous is another word for _____past_____.

4. The bus (fare) from Cedar Road to the street (fair) is affordable.
   Payment is another word for _____fare_____.

5. The (scene) from your window is the most lovely I've ever (seen).
   Viewed is another word for _____seen_____.

6. After he (threw) out the trash, Marlon was (through) with her chores.
   Finished is another word for _____through_____.

7. What's the best (way) to (weigh) a toddler who won't sit still?
   Method is another word for _____way_____.

8. The bus driver almost (missed) the exit to the farm because of the (mist).
   Overlooked is another word for _____missed_____.

80

Conquer Grammar • Grade 6 • © Newmark Learning, LLC

Page 81

Homophones

Homophones are words that sound the same but have different spellings and meanings. Some examples of homophones include contractions and possessive pronouns like the following: **they're/their, it's/its, you're/your, who's/whose**.

Contraction	Possessive Pronoun
they're = they are	their
it's = it is	its
you're = you are	your
who's = who is	whose

Write the contraction and the possessive pronoun of the words in the parentheses ( ) on the correct line to complete each sentence.

1. I know that _____you're_____ very busy, but I could use your _____your_____ help. (you are)

2. The students think _____they're_____ going to miss the start of school because _____their_____ bus is late. (they are)

3. Do you know _____who's_____ playing in the football game tonight? (who is)

4. _____It's_____ fun to watch my cat chasing _____its_____ tail. (it is)

5. Please raise _____your_____ hand if _____you're_____ in the choir this year. (you are)

6. _____Whose_____ markers are these? _____Who's_____ missing their markers? (who is)

7. _____Who's_____ going to tell me _____whose_____ bag this is? (who is)

8. I can't tell if _____you're_____ having a good time or if you would rather be at home in _____your_____ pajamas. (you are)

9. _____They're_____ back from _____their_____ trip. (they are)

Conquer Grammar • Grade 6 • © Newmark Learning, LLC

81

Page 82

Informal and Formal Language

Informal language consists of incomplete sentences and slang. Use informal language in friendly pieces of writing, such as an e-mail or a letter to a friend. Formal language consists of complete sentences and standard grammar. Use formal language in an essay or a letter to the editor.

Informal	Formal
Hey, wanna grab a bite to eat tonight?	I wish to extend an invitation for dinner this evening.
Jay shouted, "Yo! It's been like a million years since I saw you last!"	Jay said, "Hello, I have not seen you in a long time."

Circle whether each sentence is informal or formal.

1. Let's do something super fun after school!
   (informal)   formal

2. I wish to inquire about the meeting that will be held later this week.
   informal   (formal)

3. Rachel waved at me, and I said, "Later!"
   (informal)   formal

4. The kid in the store was like, "Are you serious?"
   (informal)   formal

5. I would appreciate your advice concerning this issue.
   informal   (formal)

6. This movie is quite long, and I have an appointment in an hour.
   informal   (formal)

82

Conquer Grammar • Grade 6 • © Newmark Learning, LLC

Page 83

Informal and Formal Language

Informal language consists of incomplete sentences and slang. Use informal language in friendly pieces of writing, such as an e-mail or a letter to a friend. Formal language consists of complete sentences and standard grammar. Use formal language in an essay or a letter to the editor.

Informal	Formal
A bunch of people went to the concert.	A group of people attended the concert.

Choose the formal word or phrase in the parentheses ( ). Write it on the line.

1. The nobles _____fully ignored_____ the needs of the common people.
   (shrugged off, fully ignored)

2. The angry mob _____shouted_____ as the nobles rode by.
   (hollered, shouted)

3. The people _____staged protests_____ when the king ignored their petition.
   (staged protests, acted up)

4. The king _____did not understand_____ why his subjects revolted.
   (didn't get, did not understand)

5. The _____citizens_____ needed new leadership.
   (citizens, folks)

6. The minister _____spoke convincingly_____ and then left the chamber.
   (spoke convincingly, had his say)

Conquer Grammar • Grade 6 • © Newmark Learning, LLC

83

Answer Key

Page 84

Name _____ Date _____

Informal and Formal Language

Informal language consists of incomplete sentences and slang. Use informal language in friendly pieces of writing, such as an e-mail or a letter to a friend. Formal language consists of complete sentences and standard grammar. Use formal language in an essay or a letter to the editor.

Informal	**Formal**
Let's get out of here!	I think that we should leave now.

Choose the formal word or phrase in the parentheses ( ). Write it on the line.

1. The leaders announced that the summit was ___successful___.
   (successful, a big hit)

2. The laws were ___considerably___ more outdated than anyone realized.
   (a lot, considerably)

3. The city council chairperson tried to ___respect___ everyone's opinion.
   (do right by, respect)

4. If the new style of uniform ___tests well___, the school will officially adopt it.
   (tests well, catches on)

5. As a sign of goodwill, the king ___declared___ a holiday.
   (said it's, declared)

6. Many people ___disapproved of___ the politician's point of view.
   (disapproved of, couldn't stand)

7. The governor realized she should ___acknowledge___ the mayor at the meeting.
   (acknowledge, say hi to)

Conquer Grammar • Grade 6 • © Newmark Learning, LLC

Page 85

Name _____ Date _____

Informal and Formal Language

Informal language consists of incomplete sentences and slang. Use informal language in friendly pieces of writing, such as an e-mail or a letter to a friend. Formal language consists of complete sentences and standard grammar. Use formal language in an essay or a letter to the editor. Avoid using contractions such as **I'm** or **won't** in formal pieces of writing.

Informal	**Formal**
Hey, I'm sorry, but Mr. Florian won't be able to make it.	I regret to inform you that Mr. Florian will not be able to attend.

Rewrite each sentence. Replace the underlined words with formal language.

Possible answers are provided.

1. <u>Huh</u>, how come the concert <u>got</u> canceled?
   I am wondering why the concert has been canceled.

2. I <u>totally love</u> flying <u>wherever.</u>
   I greatly enjoy flying to different destinations.

3. Cancun, Mexico, is a <u>sweet</u> place to visit.
   Cancun, Mexico, is a wonderful place to visit.

4. An active volcano is the <u>coolest thing</u>.
   An active volcano is an amazing sight.

5. If traveling by plane <u>isn't your thing</u>, there's <u>tons</u> to see closer to home.
   If you do not like to travel by plane, there are many places and landmarks to visit closer to home.

6. Seeing spiders in person <u>freaks me out</u>.
   Seeing spiders in person frightens me.

Conquer Grammar • Grade 6 • © Newmark Learning, LLC

Page 86

Name _____ Date _____

Informal and Formal Language

Informal language consists of incomplete sentences and slang. Use informal language in friendly pieces of writing, such as an e-mail or a letter to a friend. Formal language consists of complete sentences and standard grammar. Use formal language in an essay or a letter to the editor. Avoid using contractions such as **I'm** or **won't** in formal pieces of writing.

Informal	**Formal**
You've really got to move a lot to stay in shape.	People need to exercise often to stay healthy.

Rewrite each sentence. Replace the informal language with formal language.

Possible answers are provided.

1. Think you don't need exercise? You're totally wrong.
   You may think exercise isn't necessary, but that is not true.

2. Exercise is super good for your heart.
   Exercise benefits your heart.

3. A good workout leaves you feeling a lot more mellow.
   A good workout makes you feel much more relaxed.

4. Working out is a really awesome way to get fit.
   Working out is an excellent way to become fit.

5. If using machines isn't your thing, chill out and find another way to work out.
   If you do not like using machines, it is not hard to find another way to work out.

6. You can read loads of books as you cycle on the stationary bike.
   You can read many books while you cycle on the stationary bike.

Conquer Grammar • Grade 6 • © Newmark Learning, LLC

Page 87

Name _____ Date _____

Informal and Formal Language

Informal language consists of incomplete sentences and slang. Use informal language in friendly pieces of writing, such as an e-mail or a letter to a friend. Formal language consists of complete sentences and standard grammar. Use formal language in an essay or a letter to the editor. Avoid using contractions such as **I'm** or **won't** in formal pieces of writing.

Informal	**Formal**
The sixth-grade kids brought in lots of muffins for the bake sale.	The sixth-grade students brought in many muffins for the bake sale.

Rewrite each sentence. Replace the informal language with formal language.

Possible answers are provided.

1. Wow, the cop who spoke at our school today was awesome.
   The police officer who spoke at our school today was excellent.

2. All the kids thought the stuff she said was cool.
   All the students thought the information she presented was very helpful.

3. Did you learn a heap from her talk?
   Did you learn a great deal from her presentation?

4. Sophie's dad works at the fire station a couple of blocks away.
   Sophie's father works at the fire station that is two blocks away.

5. If we send him an invite to our class, I'm guessing he'd show up.
   If we invite him to our class, I think he would accept.

6. Man, I want to know literally all the info about being a firefighter.
   I would very much like to know the facts about being a firefighter.

Conquer Grammar • Grade 6 • © Newmark Learning, LLC

Answer Key

Page 88

Standard English

Standard English is the language used in academic writing and in classrooms. It follows accepted rules of grammar, punctuation, spelling, and vocabulary. Nonstandard or conversational English is used in informal communication, such as text messages, e-mails, and story dialogue.

Each sentence has one error in spelling, punctuation, or grammar. Rewrite each sentence, applying the rules of standard English.

1. Felicia wrote a letter to the editor she wants everyone to vote for her mom.

   Felicia wrote a letter to the editor. She wants everyone to vote for her mom.

2. Both Winnie and Yuki did well on her assignments.

   Both Winnie and Yuki did well on their assignments.

3. The archaeologists found rare artifacts at the new sight.

   The archaeologists found rare artifacts at the new site.

4. Gianni said that he once faced a similar problem hisself.

   Gianni said that he once faced a similar problem himself.

5. By the time the downpour began, I were at home.

   By the time the downpour began, I was at home.

6. The movie about the boy who wanted to be a firefighter.

   The movie was about the boy who wanted to be a firefighter.

7. Do you know who's snacks are on the table?

   Do you know whose snacks are on the table?

Page 89

Standard English

Standard English is the language used in academic writing and in classrooms. It follows accepted rules of grammar, punctuation, spelling, and vocabulary. Nonstandard or conversational English is used in informal communication, such as text messages, e-mails, and story dialogue.

Rewrite each sentence, applying the rules of standard English.

1. If it ain't broke, don't fix it.

   If it isn't broken, you don't need to fix it.

2. Raj finished his homework real fast because he wanted to hang out with his friends.

   Raj finished his homework quickly because he wanted to go out with his friends.

3. I need to find the article about them heroes.

   I need to read the news story about those heroes.

4. The students want that there rule about cell phones to be changed.

   The students want the rule about cell phones to be changed.

5. I think that sometimes nature be better than civilization.

   I think that sometimes nature is better than civilization.

6. My dad he claim that the 1980s were the golden age of popular music.

   My dad believes that the 1980s were the golden age of popular music.

Page 90

Standard English

Standard English is the language used in academic writing and in classrooms. It follows accepted rules of grammar, punctuation, spelling, and vocabulary. Nonstandard or conversational English is used in informal communication, such as text messages, e-mails, and story dialogue.

Rewrite the letter using standard English grammar, spelling, punctuation, and vocabulary. Errors in standard English are underlined.

Dear Editor,

    Students for Bridge Park would like to invite the entire city to come out on Sunday to support <u>are</u> local park. Bridge Park is <u>a way big</u> contributor to city life. Each year, thousands of people <u>visits</u> the park to swim, hike, or ride <u>there</u> bicycles. The <u>parks</u> many acres also support local species from historic old trees to colorful flocks of birds to a large <u>heard</u> of <u>deers</u>.

    On Sunday, our class <u>are</u> holding a picnic to raise money for Bridge Park. The money will go toward additional <u>childrens</u> activities. We hope to <u>insure</u> that the park will always be a <u>cool</u> place for people of all ages.

Sincerely,
The Sixth Grade Class

Dear Editor,

    Students for Bridge Park would like to invite the entire city to come out on Sunday to support our local park. Bridge Park is a major contributor to city life. Each year, thousands of people visit the park to swim, hike, or ride their bicycles. The park's many acres also support local species, from historic old trees, to colorful flocks of birds, to a large herd of deer.

    On Sunday, our class is holding a picnic to raise money for Bridge Park. The money will go toward additional children's activities. We hope to ensure that the park will always be a wonderful place for people of all ages.

Sincerely,

The Sixth Grade Class

Page 91

Standard English

Standard English is the language used in academic writing and in classrooms. It follows accepted rules of grammar, punctuation, spelling, and vocabulary. Nonstandard or conversational English is used in informal communication, such as text messages, e-mails, and story dialogue.

Rewrite the passage, applying the rules of standard English.

The rice paddies of china the philippines and japan is considered engineering feets of the ancient world. People have growed rice for thousands of years. About 2,000 years ago rice growers in asia began building terraced paddies. The terraces allowed the farmers to grow his rice on the sides of hills and mountains. These here terraced steps saved both space and water.

To water the rice, the farmers built a complex system of canals. The irrigation system still be used today. Water flows down the terraces, irrigating each field as it go. The young rice plants sits in fields with about six inch of water? As the rice matures, the guys can drop the water level. When the rice is ready, the ground is dry. Then the rice can be harvested nice and easy.

The rice paddies of China, the Philippines, and Japan are considered engineering feats of the ancient world. People have grown rice for thousands of years. About 2,000 years ago, rice growers in Asia began building terraced paddies. The terraces allowed the farmers to grow their rice on the sides of hills and mountains. The terraced steps saved both space and water.

To water the rice, the farmers built a complex system of canals. The irrigation system is still used today. Water flows down the terraces, irrigating each field as it goes. The young rice plants sit in fields with about six inches of water. As the rice matures, the farmers can drop the water level. When the rice is ready, the ground is dry. Then the rice can be harvested easily.